A collection of elegant yet approachable dinners, perfect for sharing with friends over a glass of wine.

Colu Cooks: Easy Fancy Food redefines everyday eating with sophisticated dishes and empowering recipes to get you out of your weeknight routine, coax you to explore new ingredients and techniques, and get a stylish meal on the table without overthinking it.

COLU COOKS

Colu Cooks

Easy *Fancy* Food

COLU HENRY

ABRAMS, NEW YORK

Editor: Holly Dolce
Managing Editor: Glenn Ramirez
Design Manager: Danielle Youngsmith
Production Manager: Kathleen Gaffney

Book and cover design by: Alaina Sullivan

Library of Congress Control Number: 2021946807

ISBN: 978-1-4197-4780-9
eISBN: 978-1-64700-671-6

Printed and bound in China
10 9 8 7 6 5 4 3 2

Abrams books are available at special discounts when
purchased in quantity for premiums and promotions as
well as fundraising or educational use. Special editions
can also be created to specification. For details, contact
specialsales@abramsbooks.com or the address below.

Abrams® is a registered trademark of Harry N. Abrams, Inc.

ABRAMS The Art of Books
195 Broadway, New York, NY 10007
abramsbooks.com

*For my Chad and
our Joshie.
You make me whole.*

Contents

Introduction

This book didn't start as a book at all, but as recipes that I was jotting down hastily on a thick sketch pad as I was cooking. (Why, of course I keep weighted paper and a felt-tip pen by the stove, don't you?) The more I flipped through the pages and began thinking of them as a collection, the more I also began to notice an organic pattern of what I was trying to convey.

Similarly to my first cookbook, *Back Pocket Pasta*, I wanted to write a personal book that inspired home cooks to make simple yet sophisticated dishes they'd feel proud of. And I hope you do and will! But I noticed something else, too. The more I wrote, the more I realized what was truly bringing me joy. It wasn't just the food; it was sharing stories through food and recipes about the people I chose to surround myself with and the places I'm lucky enough to visit.

There's something that's elemental and identifying about the way we choose to eat. I once sat next to a woman similar in age who, like me, was dining alone at the bar at L'Express in Montreal. It was noon and she was eating a half-dozen oysters while drinking a glass of Chablis and reading a book of short stories entitled *Mise en Bouche*. A kindred spirit. Whether she noticed me or not, I saw her, and I saw myself and our extended bunch, in her.

These recipes and moments reflect my life. Chad and I have chosen to be a family of two (well, three, if you count our eighteen-year-old rescue pup Joshie, which I certainly do). And whether we're gathered around our table, sitting on the front porch plates in laps, or standing in the kitchen drinks in hand, when you come over to my house for a meal, you are part of the story.

Eight years ago, we left Brooklyn and moved upstate to Hudson, New York. It was a big lifestyle shift change that didn't come without fear. I, who vowed to be the last of our friends standing in Brooklyn, was the first to leave. And now instead of taking the subway to the supermarket, I drive (white-knuckled) to a barn in Blundstone boots to pick up my winter farm share and weekly loaf of Sparrowbush Farm sesame bread. Yes, I know it sounds bucolic. It is. Since we have a lot more space and many less options for dining out, we also throw a lot of dinner parties and have friends over for drinks and snacks more often than we don't. I am cooking five to six nights a week for them, for Chad, and sometimes just for myself (an underrated pleasure in my opinion).

My food is rooted in my Italian-American upbringing, so you're going to see pastas, chicories, anchovies, olives, and citrus strewn throughout, and maybe a very special eggplant Parmesan. (Yes, you do need another recipe for one.) But my cooking is also influenced by the rich farmland of the Hudson Valley, time spent in Spain and France, the south shore of Nova Scotia, and other travels abroad. It would be remiss not to include the other beloved valleys in my life—Napa and Sonoma—which have been incredibly formative, specifically in regard to the way I approach vegetables. You will see these elements reflected throughout the book in the form of recipes that rely heavily on seasonal produce, an amply stocked pantry, and more often than not, meat used as an accessory. Of course there are some exceptions. I do love to roast a chicken (lime pickle anyone?) and serve a meat sauce that's been simmering all day, as well as a slow-roasted pork shoulder and braised lamb shanks that fall off the bone.

And while I am a very relaxed and go-with-the-flow-cook, the one thing in the kitchen I am not

is a baker. So in this book, I decided to do what I do when having people over for dinner: I called on some incredibly talented friends to "please bring dessert" and contribute their favorite simple recipes. Given the fact that I am also not a sweets person this decision to offer up some of my friends' best dessert recipes here makes a lot of sense. You don't have to be able to do everything perfectly—or even want to, for that matter—in order to get the payoff of making dinner and memories at home with people you love. (Trust me, I've worked very hard to accept this.) So even through I'm more of a savory person, who am I to deprive you of a sweet way ot end a meal? It's not very hospitable.

As you can hopefully see, I took some inspiration from 1970s *Gourmet* magazines for the aesthetic of this book; their vibe spoke to me in a big way and I listened. (I was born in the seventies, after all.) My grandmother collected *Gourmet*s starting in the 1930s, so I grew up looking at a lot of magazines. I inherited decades' worth of them in my mid-twenties, but after a few moves, Chad put his foot down and said that we would no longer be schlepping the many, many, maybe-starting-to-mildew(?) boxes to our new home in Hudson. I get it. They are now on permanent loan at the Brooklyn Kitchen, a cooking school in Industry City, if you find yourself nearby and want to take a look. I visited them when this book was beginning to take shape.

But unlike the beloved magazine in its heyday, I'm not putting any menus together. I want you to create your own, plus no one eats like that anymore! More often than not when people are coming over to my house, I'm ransacking my well-stocked pantry and farmers market–packed fridge drawers to pull something together, and that's how many of the recipe ideas in this book came about. A smoked trout dip appeared the same night as a saucy pasta and everyone was more than ok with that. Try cooking with the philosophy that you are dining out at a restaurant with friends. Someone might want the roast chicken, the steak, or the pasta, but you know everyone also really wants the tater tots (no recipe for tots in this book though; I just buy them in the freezer section and sometimes deep-fry them). So you order those too, as well as a salad for the table. Everyone just ends up sharing everything anyway. It's more fun that way. ∎

To Keep *on* Hand

13-17

In My Pantry

ALLIUMS AND GARLIC: Yellow onions, red onions, shallots, green onions, and garlic are essential to have around. They make up the backbone of a lot of meals. Additionally, onions and shallots make for a great side dish, cut into wedges and roasted on a sheet pan alongside chicken, sausage, or fish. They are also perfect for a quick pickle. Splash them with vinegar and a pinch of salt and use them as a garnish for topping salads, soups, and stews.

BEANS: I'm crazy for dried beans and specifically the ones from Rancho Gordo. I buy as many varieties as I can—white, brown, red, and black. Their taste is infinitely superior. But canned beans are also smart to have on hand as they allow you to pull together dishes quickly if you haven't thought ahead. White beans with some broth and greens make a satisfying lunch or dinner. Black beans with rice or turned into a soup with cumin and onion and a spoonful of sour cream are equally hearty. Plus so much more!

CANNED TOMATOES: Perfect for pasta and pizza sauce, they are also a dependable staple for pulling together chilies, braises, and even straight up tomato soup. My favorite brands are Bianco DiNapoli and Mutti. They can't be beat. I primarily buy cans of whole tomatoes as they tend to be better quality due to the fact that they are less processed, but I also have the occasional can of crushed or a jar of passata as well.

CHICKEN STOCK: I roast a lot of chickens and therefore make a lot of stock at home, but I also always have a box or two of the premade stuff as well. I always buy organic and low-sodium so I can be in control of the salt level. I prefer the Pacific Foods brand. Better Than Bouillon is also a great product.

NUTS: Nuts add texture when toasted and tossed in salads, add a nice crunch to roasted vegetables, and are interchangeable in pestos. I usually have unsalted almonds, walnuts, hazelnuts, and pistachios all within easy reach, but even two types will suffice.

PASTA AND NOODLES: I suggest having a few types of dried pasta in the pantry such as the long and lean varieties like linguine and bucatini, and one with texture and one with a tube, such as rigatoni and fusilli. Ideally, I also have a small cut on hand, such as ditalini or fregola, which work well for brothy soups. Asian noodles such as soba, udon, ramen, and rice noodles are also lovely for soups, salads, and stir-frys.

In My Fridge

RICE AND GRAINS: I generally have white, both long-grain and short-grain, as well as Arborio for risottos. Brown rice is good too, and for sure grab it if it's more up your alley. I also love nutty farro for the base of a grain salad as well as for many other things.

SPICES: You don't need a million spices lurking about, but you do want to make sure that they are fresh, not sitting in a drawer for over a year getting dusty for lack of use. Keep it simple and straightforward. My go-tos are Aleppo pepper, cinnamon, ground cumin, cumin seeds, coriander seeds, garam masala, red pepper flakes, fennel seeds, smoked paprika, and za'atar.

TINNED FISH: Italian tuna in olive oil! Anchovies! Sardines! Smoked trout! These can all be meals on their own served on toast, but they also oomph-up pasta dishes when sautéed with lots of garlic and olive oil, as well as make good pizza toppings. White beans stirred into some broken down anchovies in lots of oil served with a hunk of bread and a glass of wine is one of my favorites meals.

SUGARS: Light brown sugar, maple syrup, agave, and honey are great in marinades and offer a nice balance to anything salty, spicy, or both.

CONDIMENTS: Clearly you don't need to have all of these pickles, pastes, and preserves, but I do often rely on them heavily to amp up my weeknight dinner game. Here are some of my favorites: Calabrian chiles, Castelvetrano olives, chili crisp, harissa paste, Hellmann's mayonnaise, kimchi, lime pickle, Maille cornichons and Dijon mustard, miso paste, preserved lemon, Red Boat fish sauce, toasted sesame oil, soy sauce, tahini, and tomato paste.

CITRUS AND GINGER: I have an overflowing bowl in my fridge filled with lemons, limes, ruby red grapefruit, and ginger, so it's all in one place within close reach.

DAIRY: I like to have hard cheese, such as pecorino or Parmesan, both to snack on and for serving with pasta, pizza, and whatever else. Feta cheese and sour cream or crème fraîche are also nice to have for a quick dip or dollop. Unsalted butter and half-and-half are also not optional.

EGGS: Brown or white, up to you, but always large. Breakfast for dinner is never a bad idea.

Make a frittata, fry an egg and put it over leftover pasta, or poach one and put it on a grain salad. If you have eggs in the fridge you have a meal in minutes. Like vegetables and meat, buy them locally if you can.

HERBS: It's no secret that I love herbs. Not only to finish my dishes, but also in the many versions of green sauces you will see inside this book. I am never without flat-leaf parsley, cilantro, and mint. I also adore tarragon and chives. In the summer it's bushels of basil.

Near My Stove

KOSHER SALT AND BLACK PEPPER: Diamond Crystal is my go-to. If I call for a specific amount of salt in a recipe, it's using this brand. If you use Morton's it is a "saltier salt," so reduce the quantity by about half. I also use whole black peppercorns in a grinder, usually on the coarse setting. Please only use freshly ground pepper. Fin.

COOKING OILS: My everyday olive oil (of which I use plenty) is the extra-virgin California Olive Ranch brand. It's a very good quality and affordable oil. I don't look further. In addition, I keep a higher quality olive oil (not extra-virgin) from Spain or Italy, which is buttery and peppery, for finishing dishes. I also keep neutral oils such as canola, vegetable, or grapeseed nearby, as they have a higher smoking point and work well if I need to get a good sear on something. I keep both labeled in plastic squeeze bottles so I can manage how much oil I'm using. Webstaurant.com is an incredible resource for industrial kitchen needs like these, as well as bottles.

FLAKY SALT: I love finishing most dishes with a few pinches of flaky salt for seasoning and texture. My friend Ben Jacobsen makes great flaky salt, aptly under the name Jacobsen Salt Co., which is hand-harvested in Netarts Bay in Oregon. I'm partial to it, not just because he's my friend—it's just fantastic salt. Maldon from France is quite good as well.

GOOD-QUALITY VINEGARS: Katz vinegar (store.katzfarm.com), based out of the Napa Valley, is my go-to brand for apple cider, red, and white wine vinegars. Drizzle them on anything for a bright lift instead of citrus, or use them in a salad dressing. I do splurge occasionally for good-quality balsamic as well; it's so worth it. Acetaia San Giacomo, produced in Novellara, Italy, is my favorite.

CHAPTER ONE

Eat *with* Your Hands

19-41

A *Family Picnic*

My friend Tamar and I established a family picnic tradition about one year into our friendship. (In my opinion, an appropriate time to put a tradition into place, as you know you've really committed to the relationship.) Our family picnic dinner consists of odds and ends, leftover from the week, and plenty of wine.

In recent months, this tradition has also become part of our routine with our no longer "new" neighbors Chris and Kelly. Because as soon as I get the five P.M. text "Drinks?," we all know what it really means—I dust off the front porch chairs and, unrequested, take out the leftover olives I stored with the Italian artichokes in olive oil from last weekend, a wheel of already-wedged-into Camembert, a few slices of last night's pork roast or chicken, and whatever else I can forage. There is also usually something pickled. We are all very, very good wine drinkers, so one must arrive prepared with sustenance. (Luck favors those that do, so I'm told.) There are more meats, cheeses, and crackers on their end to round out this meal, and in a flash it's ten P.M. In our ever-growing friend-family, these picnics generally take place at a walkable location on a Friday or Saturday evening. But do what feels right to you. If a Monday comes around and it feels appropriate, you should most certainly lean in and embrace it. There is no "right night" to cobble together a meal with friends.

For some inspiration, please allow me to provide you with some examples of family picnics past:

One evening, I brought over roasted beets to Tamar's, the remains of a meat and cheese plate, and some eggs to soft boil. I also had some leftover homemade mayonnaise, so I brought that too. Tamar had braised beef the night before, which she gently reheated in the oven, and then dressed with garlicky chive oil and wide ribbons of Treviso radicchio. We also drizzled the eggs with the garlicky oil and some pickled chiles. The beets were tossed with

flaky salt. We combined our cheese and cured meats and put the board down in the center of the table. Her husband Pete's father had made bread, which we tore apart with our hands and sopped our plates with. In my book (now literally), it is still one of the most satisfying meals in my forty-four-year-old history.

We've also enjoyed dinners with outsourced fried chicken, complemented with homemade chicken liver mousse, roasted red peppers in olive oil with capers and herbs, cream laden polenta, and the remains of a layer cake created by the brilliant pastry chef Natasha Pickowicz. An evening of leftover, recipe-tested shrimp pâté spread onto endive leaves and smashed into our mouths is also high on the list, as is one with day-old roasted root vegetables with yogurt dressing and a side of meatballs swimming in cinnamon-spiked tomato sauce.

There are no rules for a family picnic menu (although they generally tend never to be the same twice), I just happen to host a lot of cocktail parties, which is why mine tend to be meat, cheese, and brine forward. They are all about creating merriment and the ease of entertaining with your chosen family and throwing together a simple and soulful meal that is assembled with what you have as opposed to shopping, preparing, and cooking in advance.

And, if you cook often, infrequently, or barely at all, I have faith there is always something in your fridge or pantry you can pull together to feel nourishing and special, even if it's filling a bowl full of potato chips and opening a bottle of Champagne on a stormy day to thank Mother Nature for her wild and wily ways. Wouldn't you agree?

Soft-Boiled Eggs *with* Pickled Chiles

The first time we met, Tamar wasn't sure if she would like me enough to stay for dinner, so instead she put out a large cheese board draped with mortadella and beautiful jammy eggs topped with pickled chiles, and yes, plenty of wine. Luckily I made the cut and she passed her recipe along, which inspired this one, now a staple in my household. The chiles prove to be incredibly handy when you throw a last-minute cocktail party. I bet they would actually be incredible in a martini. We also use them on pizza, sandwiches, greens, pastas, or really anywhere you want some briny heat. Tamar and I now make these pickled chiles together in the very late summer when we are up to our ears in every kind of pepper you can imagine and frantically trying to hold on to the season.

SERVES 4 to 6

(Chiles serve many, for many months)

TIME 25 minutes *(Plus a day in the fridge. But you can eat these after a few hours too)*

INGREDIENTS

1 pound (455 g) fresh chiles, such as jalapeños, serranos, cayennes, or Fresnos, thinly sliced into rounds

1¾ cups (420 ml) distilled white vinegar

2 teaspoons kosher salt, plus more to taste

2 teaspoons raw sugar, plus more to taste

FOR THE EGGS:

Kosher salt

6 large eggs

Flaky salt

METHOD

Pickle the chiles: Wash two 16-ounce (480 ml) wide-mouth Mason jars with lids well with hot, soapy water. Add the chiles, packing them in tightly, but leave enough room at the top of the jars to close them with ease once the liquid is poured in.

In a saucepan, bring ½ cup (120 ml) water and the vinegar to a boil. Add the kosher salt and the sugar and simmer until the salt and sugar dissolve. Taste and adjust the seasonings to your liking. You may want it a bit sweeter or perhaps saltier; the journey to a perfect pickle brine is yours.

Pour the hot brine over the chiles and seal the jars tightly. Allow the jars to come to room temperature then store in the refrigerator.

Prepare the eggs: Bring a large pot of salted water to a rapid boil. Gently lower the eggs into the pot and turn down to a simmer. Cook the eggs for 7 minutes if you like them jammy; a few minutes longer if not. Drain and run under cool water to stop them from cooking further.

Peel the eggs and arrange them on a platter. Season with flaky salt and top each with a few chiles.

Buttery Kimchi Shrimp

Kimchi, a classic Korean banchan dish of salted, fermented vegetables, creates a subtle, delightfully funky sauce for sweet shrimp when stirred into melted butter. Keep in mind that some store-bought kimchis are spicier than others, so taste yours before deciding if you want to add additional heat with red pepper flakes. Although, some do like it hot . . . don't make me sing! But seriously, good brands to look for are Mother In Law's and Mama O's. Adding a generous squeeze of lime juice just before serving gives the whole dish a bright lift and really brings it together.

SERVES 4

TIME 10 minutes

INGREDIENTS

¾ cup (155 g) roughly chopped kimchi (see brand recommendations above)

1½ pounds (680 g) jumbo shrimp, peeled and deveined, tails removed if you like

Kosher salt

3 tablespoons (40 g) unsalted butter

2 cloves garlic, finely chopped

2 teaspoons thinly sliced fresh ginger

½ teaspoon red pepper flakes (optional)

½ lime, for serving

2 tablespoons roughly chopped fresh cilantro, for garnish

Flaky salt, for finishing (optional)

METHOD

Finely chop the kimchi until it resembles a coarse paste. Season the shrimp with kosher salt.

In a 12-inch (30.5 cm) skillet, melt the butter over medium heat. Stir in the garlic, ginger, and red pepper flakes, if using, and cook until fragrant, about 1 minute. Add half the shrimp to the pan in one layer and cook undisturbed until they just start turning pink, about 1 minute. Flip and cook for about 1 minute more, transfer to a plate, and set aside. They may not be fully cooked at this time—that's OK. Repeat with the remaining shrimp.

Return all the shrimp to the pan with any juices that have accumulated. Add the kimchi paste and stir together until the shrimp is well coated and cooked through, about 1 to 2 minutes more.

Arrange the shrimp in a bowl or on a plate. Squeeze the lime and scatter the cilantro over the top. Season with flaky salt, if desired, and make sure to spoon the residual pan sauce over the top.

Smoky Trout Dip *for* Reed

My good friend Reed is an Alabama native who, lucky for me, ended up in the town of Hudson, New York, for a spell. An avid fisherman and forager, he's known for taking solo voyages around Columbia County searching for fiddlehead ferns, brook trout, and whatever else happens to be in season. He once left a ramp bouquet on my front porch Easter morning (no note!). I mean, come on. We cook together when we can and he is crazy for smoked trout, which he eats with eggs for breakfast numerous times a week. I've created a southern-leaning dip in his honor as he's also cuckoo for rémoulade, a condiment used frequently alongside low-country cooking. Serve with a sleeve of saltines or alongside crisp vegetables such as fennel, radishes, or celery.

SERVES 4 to 6

TIME 10 minutes

INGREDIENTS

6 ounces (170 g) smoked trout, skin and bones removed

¼ cup (60 ml) crème fraîche or sour cream

2 tablespoons mayonnaise

2 tablespoons roughly chopped capers

2 tablespoons finely chopped bread and butter pickles

2 tablespoons roughly chopped fresh dill

Kosher salt and freshly ground black pepper

Lemon wedge, for finishing

METHOD

In a medium bowl, add the trout, crème fraîche, mayonnaise, capers, pickles, and half the dill. Gently stir together with a fork until the fish is flaked and everything is well combined.

Taste, and if needed, season with salt (the smoked fish can already be pretty salty, as are the capers), black pepper, and a squeeze of lemon.

Transfer the dip to a ramekin or small bowl and top with the remaining dill if serving right away. If not, the dip can be made 2 days in advance and topped with the fresh herbs right before serving.

Fancy Toast

Things on toast just taste better. It is reliable, delicious, and easy to prepare. I adore it underneath a bowl of brothy beans. It is comforting after I've braised all day and am still too darn lazy to make potatoes, or really anytime I need a warm, buttery snack.

One summer we spent many a weekend at Chad's studio in Ghent. With only a hammock and a grill the two of us put together some pretty lovely meals, and I coined the term "fancy toast," which simply means piling ingredients you generally utilize in other ways on top of grilled bread. Here are some of my favorite examples, and no, you need not a grill nor a hammock to assemble them.

Broccoli Rabe Toast *with* Melted Provolone

SERVES 4 to 6

TIME 35 minutes

INGREDIENTS

Kosher salt

1 bunch broccoli rabe, cut into ½-inch (12 mm) pieces

3 tablespoons olive oil

4 to 5 oil-packed anchovy fillets

2 cloves garlic, finely chopped

2 Calabrian chiles, thinly sliced, or ½ teaspoon red pepper flakes

½ teaspoon lemon zest

3 ounces (85 g) freshly grated extra-sharp provolone

6 slices (¾ inch/2 cm thick) crusty country bread or boule

METHOD

Bring a large pot of salted water to a boil and blanch the broccoli rabe for 3 to 4 minutes. You want it on the softer side, so "over-blanching" is a head start that will save you time in the pan. Drain the broccoli rabe.

Heat the olive oil in a 12-inch (30.5 cm) deep-sided skillet over medium heat. Add the anchovies, garlic, and chiles and cook until the anchovies have melted and the garlic is fragrant, 1 to 2 minutes. Add in the broccoli rabe and cook, stirring occasionally, until it's cooked down and very tender, adding in a tablespoon or two of water if needed to help it along. Stir in the lemon zest.

While the broccoli rabe cooks, preheat the oven to broil. Arrange the bread slices in a single layer on a sheet pan and toast until golden, about 2 to 3 minutes per side. Remove from the oven and top each toast evenly with the broccoli mixture. Sprinkle each toast evenly with the grated provolone and return to the oven to broil until the cheese melts and turns golden in spots, about 2 to 3 minutes more, watching closely to make sure the toasts don't burn. Serve whole or cut in half and eat with gusto.

Lemony Anchovy Toast *with* Radishes and Herbs

I can't in good faith give you an actual recipe for anchovy toast with butter, lemon, and herbs. You are all very smart readers and I trust you know how to assemble. But, this is a cookbook and so I shall share some suggestions on how to make *presentation-worthy* anchovy toast.

Take out a stick of unsalted butter, place it on a dish, and let it sit until it's at room temperature. Zest a Meyer lemon or regular lemon all over the top of that butter and give it a few good turns of coarse black pepper from the pepper mill. Pull out a pretty can or jar or two of imported Italian or Spanish anchovies packed in oil and set it next to the butter. Next to that, place bowls of thinly sliced radishes and tender herbs such as parsley, chives, or chervil and maybe some caper berries if you're feeling festive. Now toast some of your favorite bread and put that out too. If you're feeling generous of spirit, a few different kinds are nice, but not necessary. I always lean toward a sesame-seeded loaf as I am an Italian zia at heart. Supply butter knives and some napkins and send your guests to the table to build their own towers of toast.

If you feel like putting out other tinned fish such as sardines, smoked mussels, or razor clams, that's very nice of you indeed, and I'm sure this would be welcomed. You will then need some small forks and plates to accompany this spread and perhaps a few lemon wedges. No big deal. You've got this.

And while you've slyly put your friends to work on constructing their own pre-dinner snack, you can quietly step away to finish warming up whatever you've cooked (obviously earlier in the day, we are professionals here). This is also an opportunity to continue drinking your very large glass of wine alone for a few moments in the kitchen before you resume hosting duties for the evening. You are very welcome.

Ricotta, 'Nduja, and Mint *on* Toast

SERVES 4 to 6

TIME 15 minutes

INGREDIENTS

¾ cup (185 g) ricotta or other soft spreadable cheese, at room temperature

Kosher salt and freshly ground black pepper

6 slices (¾ inch/2 cm) crusty country bread or boule

Olive oil, for drizzling

3 to 4 ounces (85 to 115 g) 'nduja (a spicy, spreadable sausage from Calabria), at room temperature

3 tablespoons torn or roughly chopped fresh mint

Flaky salt, for finishing

METHOD

In a small bowl, season the ricotta with salt and pepper, stirring to combine.

Preheat the oven to broil. Arrange the bread slices in a single layer on a rimmed baking sheet and drizzle both sides with olive oil. Toast until golden, checking to make sure the bread is not burning, about 2 to 3 minutes per side.

Spread the ricotta on each piece of toast, dividing it evenly, and repeat with the 'nduja. Top with the mint and drizzle each toast with additional oil and flaky salt if you please.

Asparagus, Farmer Cheese, *and* Salsa Verde

SERVES 4 to 6

TIME 20 minutes

INGREDIENTS

¼ cup (25 g) thinly sliced green garlic or the white part of green onions

2 tablespoons finely chopped fresh flat-leaf parsley

2 tablespoons finely chopped fresh mint

2 tablespoons finely chopped garlic chives or regular chives

½ cup (120 ml) olive oil, plus more for the asparagus and the toast

1 lemon halved, plus more to taste

Kosher salt

1 bunch asparagus, woody ends snapped off

6 slices (¾ inch/2 cm) crusty country bread or boule

¾ cup (85 g) farmer cheese, chèvre, or other soft, mild spreadable goat cheese

Flaky salt, for finishing

METHOD

In a medium bowl, combine the green garlic, parsley, mint, and garlic chives. Stir in the olive oil, add a good squeeze of lemon juice, and season to taste with salt, adjusting flavors to taste as needed with more lemon juice or salt.

Heat a grill pan over high heat (or alternatively use a gas or charcoal grill). Toss the asparagus lightly in olive oil (about 2 tablespoons) and season with salt and pepper. Grill, turning occasionally, until the asparagus is tender and charred, 2 to 3 minutes, depending on the fatness of your stalks. Set aside on a plate. When cool enough to touch, roughly chop the asparagus into 1-inch (2.5 cm) pieces.

Drizzle both sides of the bread with a bit of olive oil and grill until toasted, 1 to 2 minutes per side.

Spread the bread with the cheese, dividing it evenly, and top each slice with the asparagus. Spoon some of the salsa verde over the top and season with flaky salt, if you like. Use any remaining sauce over grilled fish, chicken, or steak; it will keep in an airtight container in the refrigerator for up to a week.

Guvie's Ramos Gin Fizz

Our friends Jenn and Steve throw a big New Year's Day party every year with ham and black-eyed peas for good luck. It's now a beloved tradition to bundle up, with bowls of beans and ham in hand, and stand around their fire pit to usher in the first day of the year with friends that are family. We are all usually a bit bleary eyed and headachey, but spirits are high. In recent years, Steve added a new menu item—his dad Guvie's version of the classic Ramos gin fizz cocktail. In their California home this is a Christmas Day tradition, which means a big brunch with Guvie in the kitchen shaking up drinks for the entire family, which start flowing around ten A.M. Cheers to all that.

SERVES 1 (*but can easily be batched*)

TIME 5 minutes

INGREDIENTS

1½ ounces (45 ml) gin, such as Old Tom or Plymouth

1 ounce (30 ml) heavy cream

1 raw egg white

¾ ounce simple syrup, or 1 tablespoon superfine sugar

½ ounce fresh lime juice

½ ounce fresh lemon juice

2 dashes orange flower water

1 cup (240 ml) ice cubes

1 ounce (30 ml) sparkling water

METHOD

Put the gin, cream, simple syrup, lime and lemon juices, and flower water in a cocktail shaker and dry shake (without ice) for 2 minutes.

Add the ice and shake for an additional 2 minutes, more if you can, or until you can't stand to shake anymore.

Strain into a coupe glass, top with the soda water, and serve.

A NOTE: *I left Guvie's instructions for shaking in the recipe as they were written because I love them. But, your drink will taste delightful even if you don't have the arm strength to shake for the full 2 minutes after adding the ice; 1 minute would probably be ok. Traditionally the drink is served in a Collins glass, but Steve served it to me in a coupe and I think it's, well, rather joyful, so I call for it here. Serve in whatever glass makes you happy.*

Green Goddess Dip
with Celery Leaves Instead

When the world began to self-distance in spring 2020, I started to become a lot closer to sour cream and celery leaves. I wanted them in and on everything, not necessarily together, but in this case they play very nicely. During the shelter-in-place period I even started growing celery on my windowsill in the kitchen along with green onions, much like everyone else who learned the brilliant hack from the wonderful Melissa Clark—my only attempt at "urban" gardening to date. So if you find yourself not being able to leave the house for months on end, you can likely make this dip! The herbs here (except the celery leaves, of course) are merely a suggestion; feel free to swap in mint, basil, tarragon, chervil, or whatever you like. Kelly Mariani, my friend and chef at Scribe, taught me her trick of also adding in avocado. It makes the dip even creamier, which was a texture I was desperately craving when I came up with this recipe. In retrospect, I realized it was because somehow it offered me some comfort.

SERVES 4

TIME 15 minutes

INGREDIENTS

½ cup (15 g) loosely packed celery leaves

½ cup (15 g) loosely packed fresh flat-leaf parsley (both leaves and tender stems)

2 tablespoons chives or green onions (green parts only)

2 tablespoons roughly chopped dill

2 oil-packed anchovies

1 clove garlic, roughly chopped

⅓ cup (75 ml) mayonnaise

¼ cup (60 ml) sour cream or full-fat Greek yogurt

1 medium ripe Hass avocado, pitted and peeled

3 tablespoons fresh lemon juice, plus more to taste

Kosher salt and freshly ground black pepper

Vegetables for dipping, such as little gems, fennel, radishes, asparagus, carrots, green beans, and, of course, potato chips

METHOD

In a food processor, pulse together the celery leaves, parsley, chives, dill, anchovies, and garlic until finely chopped.

Transfer the mixture to a medium bowl and stir in the mayonnaise, sour cream, and the avocado and mix together until everything is smooth and well combined.

Stir in the lemon juice and season with salt and pepper. Taste and adjust seasonings, accordingly adding more lemon juice and salt to your preference.

A NOTE: *This is a fantastic snacking dip, but it also will work well alongside grilled or roasted meat and fish or even tossed with new potatoes that have been boiled in well salted water until tender.*

Sautéed Baby Artichokes *with* Fried Jamón

This dish is inspired by a sun-drenched trip to Spain where Chad and I explored the Sherry Triangle with some dear friends for two weeks. It remains one of my favorite vacations ever. A day trip took us to the sweeping town of Ronda and to a delicious lunch of baby artichokes and fried jamón, which I downed with many glasses of fino—a trio of my very favorite things. Baby artichokes are hard to find on the East Coast (they are also much less fussy to prep, which is always a plus in my book), so when I see them in stores I snatch them up to make this dish and pretend that I am back in Spain. Crusty bread for dipping in the leftover pools of olive oil is never a bad idea.

SERVES 4

TIME 30 minutes

INGREDIENTS

1 lemon

2 pounds (910 g) baby artichokes

3 tablespoons olive oil

4 ounces (115 g) jamón or prosciutto, roughly chopped or torn into bite-size pieces

Kosher salt

Flaky salt

Good-quality olive oil, for drizzling (optional)

Crusty bread for serving (optional)

METHOD

Fill a medium mixing bowl with cold water and the juice of half the lemon. With a paring knife, trim the stem of the artichoke and cut off the top third of its leaves. Then snap the remaining dark green leaves until you're left only with the pale, green tender ones. Slice the artichoke in half lengthwise and add to the acidulated water, which will help keep it from turning brown. Repeat with the remaining artichokes.

Bring a large saucepan of water to a boil. Drain the artichokes and blanch them in the boiling water for 2 minutes. Drain, set aside, and pat dry.

Heat the olive oil in a 12-inch (30.5 cm) skillet over medium heat. When it shimmers add the jamón and cook, stirring occasionally, until it begins to crisp and brown in spots, 2 to 3 minutes. Remove from the skillet with a slotted spoon and place on a paper towel–lined plate.

Add the artichokes to the skillet and stir to coat them in the pork-cured oil. Cook, stirring frequently, for 4 to 5 more minutes until they are tender and slightly golden. Stir in the crisped jamón. Season with kosher salt to taste.

Transfer the artichokes to a medium bowl or small platter and, using the remaining half lemon, add a squeeze of lemon juice and adjust the seasoning with flaky salt as needed. Drizzle with some good-quality olive oil if you like. (You would like!)

Cozze, Cecci, Chorizo

Three of my favorite C-lettered ingredients are utilized in one dish. Fresh chorizo sausage is used as the base of a sauce to steam mussels. Fresh (or Mexican) chorizo is more like your typical Italian sausage, except it's flavored with dried chile peppers, such as guajillo and ancho, and it too needs to be cooked before eating. The Spanish variety is cured, making it good to slice and snack on. I chose the former because I like the way the crisped brown bits of pork get caught in the mussel shells, as do the chickpeas, which are tossed in to warm through just before serving. It's fun to eat. Serve to start or with a green salad and crusty bread for a full meal.

SERVES 4

TIME 25 minutes

INGREDIENTS

2 tablespoons olive oil

8 ounces (225 g) fresh chorizo sausage, casings removed

1 medium shallot, thinly sliced into rings

2 cloves garlic, thinly sliced

Kosher salt

2 pounds (910 g) mussels, scrubbed and debearded

½ cup (120 ml) white wine

1 can (15 ounces/430 g) chickpeas, drained and rinsed

3 tablespoons roughly chopped fresh flat-leaf parsley

Lemon, for finishing

Toasted bread, for serving

METHOD

In a large Dutch oven or deep-sided skillet with a lid, heat the olive oil over medium heat. Add the sausage and cook, stirring and breaking up the meat with a spoon, until browned, 5 to 7 minutes. Add the shallot and the garlic and cook until the garlic is fragrant and the shallot has softened, 2 to 3 minutes. Season with salt.

Add the mussels and the white wine and bring to a simmer. Cover and cook until the mussels pop open, 3 to 5 minutes.

Turn off the heat and stir in the chickpeas until warmed through. Transfer the mixture to a deep bowl or bowls, discarding any mussels that have not opened. Scatter with parsley and squeeze with lemon.

CHAPTER TWO

For Embellishment

43-55

For Embellishment

There are nights when the thought of conjuring up a clever new way to roast a chicken or grill a pork chop leaves me feeling burdened. I want the payoff of an intensely flavored dish, but quite frankly don't have it in me to put the time in. So instead I keep it simple and season whatever is on deck with olive oil or butter and salt and pepper. I'll then turn to my fridge and begin to poke around, my hands reaching for hastily labeled glass jars that used to contain mustard or jam and have been repurposed and filled with an assortment of punchy, creamy, herby, and bright sauces or spreads. I line them up in a row on my worn marble countertop and uncap them, assigning small, considered spoons to each. We still must make this an occasion.

While the chicken or meat or seafood cooks, I'll decide what direction I'd like to take my meal. Sometimes it's many. These *très bien assaisonnements*, or accoutrements, also reinvent leftovers. I've stirred teaspoons of whatever herb-and-nut pesto into my farro soup from earlier in the week and felt renewed. Drizzling crispy chili oil over last night's rice with a fried egg makes breakfast victorious. It's also good spooned atop farmer cheese and cold pizza. Roasted tomatillo salsa over yesterday's perhaps cumin-roasted salmon? Why not? I hope you see where I'm going here. With this I present some ideas and recipes for condiments to keep in your fridge to up your weeknight dinner game.

Crispy Garlic Chili Oil *with* Shallots and Fennel Seeds

This oil is addictively good. It's grand drizzled over roasted vegetables or fish, your portion of pasta, a fried egg, or on top of quickly seared thin slices of beef. I'm sure you'll find countless other ways to use it.

MAKES about 1½ cups (360 ml)

TIME 30 minutes

INGREDIENTS

10 large cloves garlic, finely chopped

1 cup (100 g) thinly sliced shallots (from about 2 large shallots)

1½ cups (360 ml) canola, vegetable, or grapeseed oil, plus more if needed

4 to 5 teaspoons red pepper flakes, depending on how hot you like things

3 teaspoons fennel seeds

½ teaspoon kosher salt, plus more to taste

METHOD

Put the garlic and shallots in a medium saucepan and pour in the oil. You want the aromatics just submerged in the oil, so add a teaspoon or so more oil if needed. Bring the mixture to a steady simmer over medium-low low heat. Cook, stirring frequently, until the garlic and the shallots begin to take on a golden color, 13 to 15 minutes; watch it carefully so they don't start to turn too brown or burn.

Stir in the red pepper flakes and the fennel seeds and cook, continuing to stir until they are toasted and fragrant and your house smells very, very good, 2 to 3 minutes more.

Remove from the heat and allow the mixture to cool for 10 to 15 minutes. The mixture will likely take on additional color while off the heat—that's OK. Stir in the salt, taste, and add more if you please. Allow the oil to come to room temperature and store in an airtight container in the refrigerator for up to 3 to 4 weeks.

Aioli *with* Options

Making your own aioli takes patience, a trait for which I am not known, but when the task is complete, it is well worth the reward. Go incredibly slow (slower than you think) when adding in the oil to help avoid breaking the emulsification. I've broken a few aiolis in my time and it's no fun to try and mend them, especially for that poor arm that's been relentlessly whisking away as you pray that it won't break. This recipe is for a classic, creamy, and bright version, but I've also offered suggestions on ingredients that would make nice additions should you choose to add them.

MAKES about ½ cup (120 ml)

TIME 20 minutes, give or take

INGREDIENTS

1 egg yolk, at room temperature

1 clove garlic, grated or pressed

2 teaspoons fresh lemon juice, plus more if needed

¼ teaspoon salt, plus more to taste

1 cup (240 ml) olive oil or canola oil or a combination of both

METHOD

In a metal bowl, whisk together the egg yolk, garlic, salt, and lemon juice.

In a very slow, steady stream (starting with mere drops), patiently whisk in the oil until it thickens and emulsifies. If it becomes too thick, add in a few drops of cold water or lemon juice and keep going. If the mixture looks too thin, whisk without adding additional oil for a minute or so.

Once all the oil has been emulsified, taste and season with more salt and lemon juice if needed. Store in an airtight container in the refrigerator for up to a week.

OPTIONS: *Stir in a spoonful of harissa, horseradish, pesto, curry powder, finely chopped preserved lemon, or finely chopped herbs, such as tarragon, parsley, or chives.*

Whatever Herb *and* Nut Pesto

Pesto is not just perfect tossed with pasta, I promise. It works beautifully spooned over a piece of fish with a squeeze of lemon, used as a dip, whooshed on a plate and topped with caprese salad, or tossed with grilled string beans or really any vegetable you please.

MAKES about ⅔ cup (158 ml)

TIME 10 minutes

INGREDIENTS

2 cloves garlic

2 cups (80 g) tightly packed greens, such as basil, arugula, spinach, parsley, mint, or any other tender greens or a combination of a bunch

2 tablespoons nuts, such as walnuts, pine nuts, almonds, hazelnuts, or macadamia

½ cup (120 ml) olive oil

¾ cup (70 g) freshly grated Parmesan or Grana Padano cheese

Kosher salt

METHOD

In a food processor, pulse together the garlic, greens, and nuts until all the ingredients are roughly chopped.

In a slow steady stream, add the olive oil while pulsing the mixture. Continue until all the oil has been added and the mixture forms a loose paste.

Transfer to a bowl and fold in the cheese. Taste and adjust seasoning accordingly with salt.

Roasted Tomatillo Salsa

Making this homemade salsa takes no time at all. I make it frequently when tomatillos are in season. Yes, of course it works well on tacos, and as a dip for chips, but it's also delicious on grilled seafood and meat or stirred into beans.

MAKES about 2 cups (480 ml)

TIME 15 minutes

INGREDIENTS

1½ pounds (680 g) fresh tomatillos, husks removed, rinsed to remove stickiness, and cut in half if large

2 small jalapeño peppers, cut lengthwise, seeds and stems removed

1 small white or yellow onion, halved

½ cup (20 g) loosely packed fresh cilantro (both leaves and tender stems)

Kosher salt

METHOD

Place the oven rack 1 to 2 inches (2.5 to 5 cm) below the heat source and set the oven to broil.

On a large sheet pan, spread out the tomatillos, jalapeños, and the onion, cut side down, in a single layer. Broil, turning the vegetables once or twice, until the tomatillos begin to release their liquid and everything becomes slightly charred, 5 to 7 minutes. Allow to cool slightly.

Transfer the mixture, along with any liquid that's been released, to a food processor or blender and add the cilantro and a good pinch of salt. Pulse until the salsa is smooth.

Transfer to a serving bowl, taste, and adjust seasoning with salt to taste.

Another Green Sauce

This one is briny, pleasantly salty, and bright, and leans Italian, just like me. I like cooking "on their way out" eggplant and zucchini slowly in a generous amount of olive oil until they are just about caramelized, and then drizzling this sauce on top. Use it anywhere.

MAKES about 1 cup (240 ml)

TIME 10 minutes

INGREDIENTS

2 cups (100 g) roughly chopped fresh flat-leaf parsley (both leaves and tender stems)

2 cloves garlic

4 anchovies, packed in oil, drained

2 tablespoons capers, rinsed well if in salt

⅔ cup (165 ml) olive oil

1 lemon halved

Kosher salt

METHOD

In a food processor or blender, pulse together the parsley, garlic, anchovies, and capers until they form a paste-like consistency.

Add the olive oil and pulse again until everything is emulsified.

Transfer the sauce to a bowl and add lemon juice and salt to taste.

Spicy Sauce *with* Cilantro, Mint, Ginger, and Lime *(Yes, It's Also Green)*

This sauce is loosely inspired by green chutney, a condiment found frequently in Indian cuisine. I like spooning it over grilled chicken or fish. It could also be used as a marinade or stirred into full-fat yogurt and served alongside crudité.

MAKES about 1 cup (240 ml)

TIME 10 minutes

INGREDIENTS

1 bunch cilantro (both leaves and tender stems), roughly chopped and loosely packed (about 2 cups/80 g)

½ cup (25 g) loosely packed fresh mint leaves

1 serrano pepper, roughly chopped

1 (2-inch/5 cm) piece fresh ginger, peeled and roughly chopped

1 clove garlic

½ cup (120 ml) neutral oil, such as grapeseed oil

1 teaspoon fish sauce

1 tablespoon fresh lime juice, plus more if needed

Kosher salt

METHOD

In a food processor or blender, pulse together the cilantro, mint, serrano pepper, garlic, and ginger until they form a paste-like consistency.

Add the oil and pulse again until everything is emulsified.

Transfer the mixture to a bowl, stir in the fish sauce and lime juice, and season with salt to taste, adding in a bit more lime juice if needed.

Artichoke and Green Olive Tapenade *with* Grapefruit

This dip is inspired by Provence, a place I love very much. For a few summers, I was lucky enough to be able to visit for a few weeks at a time. In my opinion, there is no joy greater than wandering the vast food markets and picking up ingredients for lunch and dinner. I was particularly full of awe for a stall in Pélissanne that sold an incredible variety of tapenades. Of course I tried as many as I could. I re-created my own version here. You can use it as part of a snack board, as a dip, as a spread on a sandwich, or stirred in pasta.

MAKES about 2 cups (480 ml)

TIME 10 minutes

INGREDIENTS

1 can (14 ounces/400 g) artichoke hearts, drained

1 cup (155 g) pitted Castelvetrano olives

1 clove garlic

¼ cup (13 g) roughly chopped fresh flat-leaf parsley

1 tablespoon fresh grapefruit or orange juice, plus more if needed

½ cup (120 ml) olive oil

Kosher salt and freshly ground black pepper

METHOD

In a food processor or blender, pulse together the artichokes, olives, garlic, and parsley, until they form a paste-like consistency.

Add the olive oil and pulse again until everything is emulsified.

Transfer the purée to a bowl, stir in the orange juice, and season with salt and pepper to taste, adding in a bit more citrus juice if needed.

Kinda Caponata

There are endless versions and possibilities with this classic Sicilian dish, and although many recipes call for celery (a vegetable I've learned to love), I opted to leave it out here. I wanted to concentrate on the richness of the layers of eggplant, peppers, and tomatoes and felt celery would be a detractor, but that's just me. If you can, make this a day ahead of time so the flavors can become well acquainted. Be sure to serve this caponata either warm or at room temperature. Pack it on a picnic, top your toast, or add it to your happy hour cheese plate.

MAKES about 2½ cups (600 ml)

TIME 30 minutes

INGREDIENTS

1½ tablespoons pine nuts

7 tablespoons (105 ml) olive oil, plus more for drizzling

12 ounces (340 g) eggplant, cut into ½-inch (12 mm) dice

Kosher salt

1 red bell pepper, cut into ½-inch (12 mm) dice

½ small red onion, thinly sliced

2 cloves garlic, thinly sliced

1 tablespoon tomato paste

3 ounces (85 g) cherry tomatoes or ½ medium tomato, core removed and roughly chopped

¼ cup (40 g) green olives, such as Castelvetrano, pitted and roughly chopped

1 teaspoon light brown sugar

1½ tablespoons good-quality apple cider vinegar, such as Katz's Gravenstein vinegar

1 small handful fresh basil leaves, tightly rolled and cut into thin ribbons

METHOD

Toast the pine nuts in a skillet over medium heat, stirring frequently, until they begin to turn golden and toasted in spots, 2 to 3 minutes. Set aside.

Heat a 12-inch (30.5 cm) skillet over medium heat and add 5 tablespoons (75 ml) of the olive oil. When it shimmers, add the eggplant in one layer (you may need to do this in two batches) and cook, stirring occasionally, until it turns golden and crispy in spots, 8 to 10 minutes. Using a slotted spoon, transfer to a paper-towel lined plate and season with salt.

Heat the remaining 2 tablespoons (30 ml) oil in the skillet, add the peppers, onion, and garlic, and cook for 2 to 3 minutes until they begin to soften. Add the tomato paste to the pan, toast it for 1 minute, and then stir it into the mixture. Add the cherry tomatoes and cook until they begin to burst, helping them along if needed with the back of a spoon or spatula, 5 to 7 minutes more. Season well with salt.

Stir in the olives, sugar, and vinegar and cook until the sugar has dissolved, 1 minute more.

Turn off the heat, add the reserved eggplant and pine nuts to the skillet, and toss until everything is well combined. Taste and adjust seasonings accordingly. Transfer to a large bowl and drizzle with more olive oil if you like. Top with the basil right before serving.

Something Blue Cheese *and* Creamy

This recipe is halfway between a dip and a dressing, so use it any which way you please. I like spooning it on top of fried chicken or onto an iceberg-wedge salad with bacon and thinly sliced quick-pickled shallots. I also may sometimes use it to dip my pizza crusts into.

MAKES about 1½ cups (360 ml)

TIME 10 minutes

INGREDIENTS

1 cup (120 ml) full-fat yogurt

¼ cup (60 ml) mayonnaise

¼ cup (60 ml) sour cream

4 ounces (115 g) blue cheese, crumbled (I like Rogue Creamery's Oregon Blue or Bayley Hazen Blue from Jasper Hill Farm.)

2 tablespoons thinly sliced green onions

Freshly squeezed lemon juice

Kosher salt and freshly ground black pepper

METHOD

In a bowl, whisk together the yogurt, mayonnaise, sour cream, blue cheese, and green onions until well combined.

Season to taste with lemon juice, a pinch of salt and a few aggressive churns of coarse black pepper. Taste and adjust the seasonings to your liking as needed.

Cherry Tomato Confit

In mid-September, I begin gracefully hoarding the last of the summer produce and perhaps enter full panic mode. I know that very soon, I'll be looking at varietals of winter squash which, while pretty, do begin to all taste the same; turnips, which I can only handle about once a season, and rutabaga, which frankly I want, well, never. And this landscape of orange, rust, and cream will go on for many, many months. In turn, I'll buy pints and pints and pints of cherry tomatoes just to say it isn't so. Some I throw into pasta sauces or salads or pop in my mouth as a snack, but the majority of the others I slowly roast with a plentiful amount of olive oil and then freeze so I can have a reminder of what I'm looking forward to a mere nine months later. They are also delicious.

MAKES about 6 cups (900 ml)

TIME 50 minutes

INGREDIENTS

3 pounds (1.4 kg) heirloom cherry tomatoes, in a variety of shapes and colors

1 cup (240 ml) virgin olive oil

1 teaspoon red pepper flakes

6 garlic cloves, smashed and peeled

Kosher salt

8 sprigs thyme or rosemary, or a combination of both

METHOD

Preheat the oven to 300°F (150°C). Place the tomatoes in two 9 by 13-inch (23 by 33 cm) baking dishes in one layer. Add the oil, red pepper flakes, and garlic and season well with salt. Stir to make sure the tomatoes are well coated in the oil. Nestle in the herbs.

Roast, stirring a couple times, until the tomatoes begin to burst and and the skins begin to look pleasantly wrinkled, 40 to 50 minutes.

Allow to come to room temperature, remove the herb sprigs, and then store in an airtight container, pouring any residual liquid over the top. They will keep in the fridge for a couple of weeks or freeze for up to 6 months.

A NOTE: *These tomatoes work well as the base of a pasta sauce, simmered and stirred into white beans or soup, or spooned over cheese on toasted bread for a snack. You could also make the Gingery Lamb Meatballs with Tomato Confit Broth and Seeded Yogurt on page 131. I would.*

Seared Savoy Cabbage with Spicy Fish Sauce Vinaigrette and Crushed Peanuts, page 77.

CHAPTER THREE

Some *Sides*

57–79

The Roasted Red Pepper Salad

These peppers symbolize a lot. I was feeling at a low point in my career a few years ago. I was burnt out on social media and lost all passion for the one thing I loved most: cooking. That same week, I was co-hosting a dinner party and firmly declared, "I will make my roasted red pepper salad!" I don't know why, it had nothing really to do with what we were eating, but I felt the urge and leaned into it. In fact, I got all Chez Panisse-y about it and spent a full afternoon devoted to patiently roasting the peppers over the gas flames. I then further roasted them in the oven till they truly collapsed, patiently rubbed the skin off each, and dutifully removed each seed. You get the idea. I really took my time. Before I knew it, I realized I had physically connected with the act of cooking again, which is what it's really all about (and then, of course, the feeding people part). It was shortly after that I began writing this book.

SERVES 4

TIME 45 minutes

INGREDIENTS

1½ pounds (680 g) medium bell peppers, preferably in a variety of colors, such as red, yellow, and orange (preferably not green)

⅓ cup (75 ml) olive oil

4 cloves garlic, very thinly sliced

2 Calabrian chiles, thinly sliced, or ½ teasoon chile flakes

1 tablespoon capers, rinsed well if in salt

Kosher salt

1 tablespoon finely chopped fresh flat-leaf parsley

1 tablespoon finely chopped fresh mint or basil or both

Flaky salt, for serving

METHOD

Preheat the oven to broil and move the oven rack to the top to sit right below it. Cut off the tops of the peppers and remove their seeds and discard them. Cut the peppers in half lengthwise, place them cut side down on a large rimmed baking sheet, and broil until the skin is charred in spots, 10 to 12 minutes, checking frequently to make sure they do not burn. Put them in a bowl and place a plate on top so they can steam; 8 to 10 minutes.

Meanwhile, make your garlic chile oil. Heat the olive oil in a saucepan over low heat. Add the garlic and the chiles and cook until the garlic is pale golden, 2 to 3 minutes. Remove from heat and allow to come to room temperature.

When cool enough to touch, rub the skins from the roasted peppers and discard them. Cut the peppers into ¼-inch-thin strips, and place them in a medium bowl. Pour the garlic chili oil over the peppers and add the capers, season with salt, and stir to combine. Allow to sit at room temperature for about 30 minutes for the flavors to get acquainted.

Arrange the peppers on a medium plate or platter, scatter with the herbs and sprinkle with flaky salt.

A NOTE: *If making ahead, store in the fridge in an airtight container without the herbs for up to a week. Bring to room temperature before serving and then garnish with the herbs. They'll lose their color otherwise.*

Roasted Mushrooms *with* Sour Cream, Herbs, and Lemon

My friend Devon Gilroy, the chef at Hotel Tivoli, runs an incredible mushroom farm here in Hudson out of an antique warehouse downtown. If you ever come to visit, I'll try to take you there; it's very special. When the pandemic hit, many of his restaurant accounts closed and he quickly pivoted, doing online orders of mushrooms for regular people like myself, and I was very eager to support. His mushrooms are the most beautiful I have ever seen and, for a good part of the spring, I happily ate mostly mushrooms, which is how this recipe came about. I roast them until they turn beautifully crisp and golden and plate them on top of a generous amount of sour cream; the opposition of textures and temperature just work. The dish is finished with a showering of your choice of herbs and my choice of lemon zest. I also like to drizzle the dish with chili or herb oil, depending on what's in my fridge. Serve alongside anything.

SERVES 4

TIME 30 minutes

INGREDIENTS

2 pounds (910 g) mushrooms, such as shiitake, cremini, oyster, or maitake, torn roughly into pieces

¼ cup (60 ml) olive oil

Kosher salt and freshly ground black pepper

½ cup (120 ml) sour cream

¼ cup (13 g) mixed herbs, such as mint, chives, parsley, and tarragon, torn or roughly chopped

1 teaspoon lemon zest

Flaky salt, for serving

Crispy Garlic Chili Oil with Shallots and Fennel Seeds (page 46) or Herb Oil (page 209), for drizzling (optional)

METHOD

Preheat the oven to 425°F (220°C).

On a large rimmed sheet pan, toss the mushrooms with the olive oil and season well with salt and pepper.

Roast, tossing halfway through, until the mushrooms have lost their liquid and they become brown and golden in spots, 15 to 20 minutes.

Meanwhile, spread the sour cream onto the bottom of a wide shallow-mouthed bowl or platter and season with salt. When the mushrooms are finished roasting, gently spoon them on top. Top with the herbs and lemon zest and season with flaky salt. Drizzle with chili or herb oil, if using. Serve right away.

Fava Bean and Cucumber Salad *with* Feta & Sumac

Fresh fava beans aren't readily available in the Hudson Valley, but Sue, one of my favorite farmers who owns and runs Blue Star Farm, has them for a week or two in mid-June and I greedily get my hands on as many as I can. Fava beans are frequently found in Mediterranean and Middle Eastern cuisines; this dish is driven by the latter and utilizes creamy feta cheese and tangy sumac for brightness. Because favas are a rarity in these parts, I like to keep the dressing preparation simple, so they can enjoy their brief yet impactful close-up. And scene.

SERVES 4

TIME 30 minutes

INGREDIENTS

1½ pounds (680 g) fresh fava beans, shelled (about 2 cups/240 g)

Kosher salt

1 English cucumber, halved lengthwise and cut into ½-inch (12 mm) dice

4 ounces (115 g) soft feta cheese, such as the French variety, crumbled

¼ cup (5 g) roughly chopped fresh dill

1 teaspoon sumac

Olive oil

1 tablespoon fresh lemon juice, plus more to taste

Freshly ground black pepper

Flaky salt

METHOD

Bring a large pot of salted water to a boil, add the fava beans, and blanch for 1 minute. Drain and run under cold water to prevent them from cooking any longer. With patience, remove and discard their skins and place the favas in a medium bowl.

Add the cucumber, feta cheese, half the dill, and half the sumac and toss everything together gently with a generous amount of olive oil and the lemon juice, and season with salt and pepper. Taste and adjust seasonings accordingly.

Top the salad with the remaining dill and dust with the remaining sumac. Season with flaky salt.

Roasted Spring Onions *with* Pistachio Mint Pangrattato

When spring onions start appearing at the market, I breathe a sigh of relief knowing that warmer weather is on the way. Roasting spring onions brings out their sweetness, the breadcrumb topping adds textural crunch, and the lemon sings brightness. Serve these alongside seafood or roast chicken, or simply fry an egg, serve it on top, and call it dinner. I have.

SERVES 4

TIME 30 minutes

INGREDIENTS

FOR THE ROASTED SPRING ONIONS:

2 bunches spring onions (about 12 ounces/340 g total)

¼ cup (60 ml) olive oil

Kosher salt and freshly ground black pepper

FOR THE PISTACHIO MINT PANGRATTATO:

1 tablespoon olive oil

⅓ cup (30 g) panko

2 tablespoons raw pistachios, finely chopped

2 teaspoons lemon zest

3 tablespoons finely chopped fresh mint or flat-leaf parsley

Flaky salt

METHOD

Roast the onions: Preheat the oven to 425°F (220°C). On a large sheet pan or in a baking dish, toss the spring onions with the olive oil and season well with the kosher salt and black pepper. Roast until the bulbs are tender and golden brown in spots and the tops are partially charred, 25 to 30 minutes, flipping the onions halfway through to ensure even cooking.

While the onions roast, prepare the breadcrumbs: Heat the olive oil in a 12-inch (30.5 cm) skillet over medium-low heat. Toast the panko in the olive oil, stirring frequently, until the breadcrumbs are golden brown, 2 to 4 minutes. Put them in a medium bowl and toss together with the pistachios, lemon zest, and mint and season with flaky salt.

When the onions are done cooking, place them on a platter and spoon the breadcrumbs over the top.

Brown-Buttered Asparagus *with* Hazelnuts and Pickled Kumquats

You might be asking yourself in what season do asparagus and kumquats meet? Well, in California, where everything is the way life should be (sorry, Maine), the tail end of citrus season coincides with the beginning of spring, and they are very happy to hang out together for a few weeks. I first made this dish when we spent a season in the Napa Valley and my produce-loving head exploded over the incredible fruits and vegetables the region has access to. In the Hudson Valley, where I live, (and in many other places too) the asparagus season is fleeting, but catch it while you can and make this dish.

SERVES 4

TIME 20 minutes

INGREDIENTS

2 tablespoons good-quality white wine vinegar or lime juice

¼ cup (85 g) thinly sliced kumquats, seeds removed (optional)

Kosher salt

1 bunch asparagus, woody ends snapped off and discarded

¼ cup (½ stick/55 g) unsalted butter

¼ cup (35 g) raw hazelnuts, roughly chopped

2 tablespoons torn fresh mint

Flaky salt (optional)

METHOD

In a small bowl, gently whisk together the vinegar, kumquats, and a pinch of salt and set aside.

Bring a large pot of well-salted water to a boil and blanch the asparagus until crisp-tender, 2 to 3 minutes. If the stalks are on the fatter side, it may take a minute more. Drain and run under cold water to stop them from overcooking and set aside.

In a large skillet, melt the butter over medium-low heat, add the hazelnuts, and cook, stirring to make sure the nuts are well coated. Watch the butter closely. Once the foam subsides, the butter will start to take on a tawny color and begin to smell nutty, around the 3-minute mark.

Turn off the heat, add the asparagus to the skillet, and toss to coat with the browned butter. Arrange on a plate or platter. Discard the vinegar and top with the kumquats and scatter with the mint. Season with flaky salt if you please.

Roasted Carrots & Fennel *with* Toasted Almonds, Olives, and Feta

I adore my winter farm share, but I admit to being overwhelmed by the amount of carrots that seem to multiply in my crisper drawer. In an exasperated effort to find ways to use them up, I offered to bring a roasted root vegetable salad to a friend's potluck. As the vegetables were roasting, I poked around my fridge and found leftover olives from the weekend's cheese board and, of course, flat-leaf parsley. Salty feta and toasted nuts for crunch also found their way into the mix. Layered with all these flavors, I was excited to be eating carrots again. Feel free to swap in parsnips, black radishes, turnips, or any other lone, forgotten root vegetable that is looking for a home. They'll be glad you found them one.

SERVES 4 to 6

TIME 40 minutes

INGREDIENTS

1½ pounds (680 g) medium carrots, peeled and halved lengthwise if large

2 medium red onions, halved and quartered

1 large fennel bulb, cut into large wedges

¼ cup (60 ml) olive oil

Kosher salt and freshly ground black pepper

½ teaspoon Aleppo pepper or red pepper flakes

½ cup (55 g) roughly chopped almonds

1 cup (155 g) pitted and roughly chopped Castelvetrano or other green olives

4 ounces (113 g) feta cheese, crumbled

½ cup (25 g) roughly chopped fresh flat-leaf parsley

Flaky salt, for serving

Lemon wedge, for serving

METHOD

Preheat the oven to 425°F (220°C). Arrange the carrots on a rimmed baking sheet and toss with half of the olive oil, making sure the carrots are spread out to ensure even browning. Season well with kosher salt, black pepper, and the Aleppo pepper. On a second baking sheet or in a large cast-iron skillet, toss the red onions and fennel with the remaining 2 tablespoons olive oil and season with kosher salt.

Roast the vegetables, tossing occasionally, until they are brown and tender. The carrots will take 20 to 25 minutes and the red onions and fennel 5 to 10 minutes more.

While the vegetables roast, toast your almonds. Heat a 10-inch (25 cm) skillet over medium-low heat. Add the almonds and toast, stirring frequently so they do not burn, 3 to 5 minutes. Remove from heat and set aside.

Allow the vegetables to cool slightly and then transfer them to a large bowl or a platter and toss to combine. Add the olives and the feta cheese and toss again. Top with the toasted almonds and the parsley and finish with flaky salt and a squeeze of lemon.

Blistered Green Beans and Tomatoes *with* Harissa Butter

Snappy greens beans and cherry tomatoes are blistered and tossed with spicy, earthy harissa (which is mildly tamed with a bit of honey and butter) and topped with shallots that have been quickly pickled in lime juice for a jolt of acidity. As this is a summer side waiting to happen, you can alternatively char your vegetables on the grill. The tomatoes won't get the same jamminess, but they will take on a bit of smokiness and taste pretty darn good.

SERVES 4

TIME 25 minutes

INGREDIENTS

¼ scant cup (about 30 g) thinly sliced shallots

3 tablespoons fresh lime juice

Kosher salt

2 tablespoons medium or hot spiced harissa paste, I like the Belazu brand

2 teaspoons honey

2 tablespoons grapeseed or canola oil

1 tablespoon olive oil

1 pound (455 g) green beans, trimmed

1 pint (290 g) cherry tomatoes

1 tablespoon unsalted butter

Flaky salt, for garnish

METHOD

In a small bowl, stir together the shallots with 2 tablespoons of the lime juice and a pinch of kosher salt. Set aside.

In a medium bowl, whisk together the harissa, honey, and remaining 1 tablespoon lime juice and season to taste with salt.

In a 12-inch (30.5 cm) skillet, heat 1 tablespoon of the grapeseed oil and the olive oil over medium-high heat. Add the green beans and cook undisturbed until they begin to blister in spots, about 2 minutes. Toss and continue to cook until all the beans are cooked through and slightly charred, about 8 minutes more. Season with salt and place in a bowl.

Heat the remaining 1 tablespoon grapeseed oil in the skillet over medium heat. Add the cherry tomatoes and cook undisturbed until they also begin to blister in spots, about 1 minute. Stir the tomatoes until they are just cooked through and some begin to burst, helping them along with the back of a spoon if needed, about 2 to 4 minutes more.

Remove the pan from the heat. Return the green beans to the pan, pour in the harissa mixture and the butter, and stir until everything is combined and the butter is melted. Transfer to a platter and scatter with the shallots and flaky salt.

Cauliflower *with* Anchovy Oil and Crispy Capers

This gal loves a brassica and particularly has a thing for roasted cauliflower. While the cauliflower cooks, the capers are basted in olive oil until they become crunchy, and then everything is tossed together in the very best oil—that is, one with anchovies and hot pepper flakes. Honestly most any vegetable does well after a quick romp around in that. This dish would also work well with its family members broccoli or Romanesco. Serve it alongside Chicken Quintiliano (page 164) or Skillet Pork Chops with Vinegar and Honey Collards (page 121) or anything you darn well please.

SERVES 4

TIME 30 minutes

INGREDIENTS

1 medium head cauliflower, cut into small florets that include the core and tender stems

⅓ cup (75 ml) olive oil

Kosher salt and freshly ground black pepper

3 tablespoons capers, rinsed well if in salt

3 cloves garlic, thinly sliced

4 anchovy fillets, roughly chopped

½ teaspoon crushed red pepper flakes

1 tablespoon lemon zest

½ cup (25 g) roughly chopped flat-leaf parsley

Flaky salt, for finishing (optional)

METHOD

Preheat the oven to 425°F (220°C). On a large-rimmed sheet pan, toss the cauliflower with half of the oil and season well with kosher salt and black pepper. Arrange the cauliflower florets in a single layer and roast until deeply golden in color, 25 to 30 minutes, tossing halfway through to ensure even browning.

When the cauliflower is about 5 minutes from being done, heat the remaining olive oil in a deep-sided 12-inch (30.5 cm) skillet over medium-high heat. Add the capers and cook, basting with the oil, until they become crispy, about 3 minutes. Remove with a slotted spoon and set aside on a paper towel–lined plate. Reduce the heat to medium. Add the garlic, anchovies, and red pepper flakes and cook for 1 to 2 minutes more, until the garlic is pale golden and the anchovies have melted into the oil.

Add the roasted cauliflower, lemon zest, and half the parsley to the skillet and toss to combine. Top with the crispy capers and remaining parsley. Taste and season with flaky salt if you like.

Ramona Sue's Skillet Cornbread
Michael Maness

Even as fifth-generation Ozarkers, a lot of our family cooking still stems from Appalachian sources. Throughout that region, this recipe has a long history with a number of variations that go many years back. But obviously cornbread is much older than that. Indigenous American science engineered corn from wild plants over nine thousand years ago. The southeastern cultures of the Cherokee, Choctaw, Creek, and Chickasaw had various corn puddings, gruels, and early types of bread that formed the basis for this dish. The next evolution of this cornbread came from field workers cooking corn mush on hoes heated in an open fire. The advent of stoves and the increasing availability of iron skillets gave rise to this version. My mother, Arkansan by birth, made this for us almost every day. My Papaw (that's what you call your grandfather where I'm from), Sewell Haney, gave my mom the highest compliment she could get by telling her she made it as good as her mother. I think he was probably wrong. She makes it better. So here is her recipe. The ingredients matter but the technique is the most important thing. It is, as the expression goes, "as old as the hills." Needless to say, you need a seriously good iron skillet. —M.M.

SERVES 4 to 6

TIME 30 minutes

INGREDIENTS

3 tablespoons vegetable oil or shortening, but best and most traditional with saved bacon drippings

1½ cups (210 g) white cornmeal—and it should be white (it keeps the cornbread lighter and less cakey than yellow)

3 tablespoons (20 g) all-purpose flour

1½ teaspoons salt

2 teaspoons baking soda

2 cups (480 ml) full-fat buttermilk, plus more if needed

1 large egg

Thinly sliced raw onions, for serving

Room-temperature butter, for serving

METHOD

Put the oil in a 12-inch (30.5 cm) well-seasoned cast-iron skillet and heat the pan in the oven until the oven temperature reaches 425°F (220°C).

Meanwhile, prep the cornbread batter. In a medium bowl, mix together the cornmeal, flour, salt, and baking soda. In a separate bowl, whisk the egg and then add the buttermilk and mix well.

(Continued)

Add the wet ingredients to the dry ingredients and stir to combine using a wooden spoon or a whisk. If your cornmeal is older or on the dry side, you might need to stir in a few additional tablespoons of buttermilk. You're looking for a non-clumpy batter that should thickly drip off your spoon, not stay stuck to it.

Carefully remove the skillet from the oven, measure out about 2 tablespoons of the hot oil, and stir it into the cornbread mixture until fully incorporated. You can also eyeball the quantity—just make sure there is some oil still left in the skillet. The hot oil will sizzle when added to the mix—that's ok.

Place the skillet back in the oven and heat for 2 to 3 minutes. You want to make sure the skillet is hot before you add the batter.

Remove the skillet from the oven and pour the batter directly into the center of the skillet and shake the pan so it is evenly distributed (alternatively, use a rubber spatula). This is important because you want the batter to spread out from the center so it forms a great crust.

Bake for 20 to 25 minutes, until a toothpick or knife inserted in the bread comes out clean.

You're looking for a "blush," a light-orange hue that you see form on the top. You should see a few cracks as well.

Remove the skillet from the oven, place a plate on top, and invert the cornbread so the crusty bottom faces up. If your skillet is seasoned well, the cornbread will drop right out. If not, it's not the end of the world. You can just cut out pieces directly from the skillet, it just won't be as crunchy, as you'll lose some crunch from the residual heat of the pan. Cut into pie-shaped pieces; serve with sliced raw onion and softened butter.

You can make this cornbread in different-sized skillets, which will give you slight variations:

A 9- or 10-inch (23 to 25 cm) skillet will give you a higher cornbread that you can slice open with a knife and butter in between the halves.

A 12-inch (30.5 cm) skillet will give you a thinner, crunchier result that you butter on one side. This is best when using the cornbread as the centerpiece of a meal, like dipping it in the pot likker of cooked greens, and/or the broth of lima beans or black-eyed peas.

A NOTE: *For an extra-special treat, mix equal parts sorghum or blackstrap molasses with room-temperature butter and slather it on your slice.*

Seared Savoy Cabbage *with* Spicy Fish Sauce Vinaigrette and Crushed Peanuts

This Thai-influenced dressing tastes good drizzled on top of anything, but I've decided to pair it with one of my favorite vegetables—savoy cabbage. With varying shades of green and crinkly leaves, not only is she easy on the eyes, she also tastes equally good cooked or raw. For this recipe, I chose to sear the wedges for deeper flavor. Alternatively, you could do this on the grill and get similar results, but I like the golden color and occasionally crispy leaves it gets from a pan sear in hot oil. Make sure to heat the pan very well before adding the oil; it will help you get the color and texture you're looking for.

SERVES 4 to 6

TIME 25 minutes

INGREDIENTS

FOR THE VINAIGRETTE:

⅓ cup (75 ml) freshly squeezed lime juice (from 2 limes)

1 green onion (both white and green parts), thinly sliced

1½ teaspoons light brown sugar

1 small jalapeño or serrano chile, thinly sliced

2 tablespoons fish sauce

1 tablespoon finely chopped fresh cilantro

1 tablespoon finely chopped fresh mint

FOR THE CABBAGE:

1 small head of savoy or green cabbage

Kosher salt

3 tablespoons canola or grapeseed oil

2 tablespoons roughly chopped dry roasted salted peanuts

1/4 cup loosely packed Thai or regular basil leaves, torn if large

METHOD

In a medium bowl, whisk together the lime juice, scallion, sugar, jalapeño, fish sauce, cilantro, and the mint and set aside.

Cut the cabbage into 8 even wedges, leaving the core intact, and season with salt.

Heat a 12-inch (30.5 cm) cast-iron skillet over medium-high heat for 3 minutes so that it gets very hot. Add the oil, and when it shimmers, add the cabbage wedges in snugly, cut side down, and cook undisturbed until they become golden in color, 3 to 5 minutes. Flip to cook on the other side.

Place the cabbage on a large platter, spoon dressing over top. Sprinkle with crushed peanuts and basil.

Coconut Rice *with* Pea Shoots and Citrusy Cashews

You know what's better than plain rice? Coconut rice with lots of toppings. Here, jasmine rice is cooked in rich, fragrant coconut milk, flecked with ginger, and topped with cashews that have been tossed with cilantro, lime, and honey and then salty, crispy shallots. It works nicely alongside the Spatchcocked Lime Pickle Roasted Chicken (page 166). Before cooking, make sure to rinse your rice a few times until the water runs clear. This removes debris and surface starch, resulting in fluffier rice.

SERVES 4

TIME 25 minutes

INGREDIENTS

3 tablespoons grapeseed or canola oil

1 (2-inch/5 cm) piece fresh ginger, peeled and thinly cut into matchsticks

1 cup (190 g) jasmine rice, rinsed well

1 cup (240 ml) canned, unsweetened coconut milk

1 teaspoon kosher salt

⅓ cup (170 g) roughly chopped roasted, unsalted cashews

⅓ cup (15 g) roughly chopped loosely packed fresh cilantro (both leaves and tender stems)

½ teaspoon lime zest

1 tablespoon fresh lime juice

¼ teaspoon honey

½ teaspoon red pepper flakes (optional)

Flaky salt

1 medium shallot, thinly sliced into rings

2 cups (170 g) pea shoots

METHOD

In a medium saucepan, heat 1 tablespoon of the oil over medium heat. Add the ginger and sauté until fragrant, 1 to 2 minutes. Add the rice and stir together. Pour in the coconut milk plus ¾ cup (175 ml) water and salt and and bring to a boil. Turn down the heat to low, cover, and cook for about 15 minutes or until the coconut milk is absorbed. Remove from heat and let rest covered for 10 minutes more.

While the rice is cooking, prepare the cashews and shallots. Toast the cashews in a skillet over medium-low heat, stirring frequently, 4 to 5 minutes. In a medium bowl, stir together the toasted cashews, cilantro, lime zest and juice, honey, and red pepper flakes if using. Season with flaky salt to taste and set aside.

Heat the remaining 2 tablespoons oil in a skillet over medium-high heat. Add the shallots and cook, stirring frequently, until golden, 3 to 5 minutes. Place on a paper towel–lined plate to drain and sprinkle with flaky salt.

Transfer the rice to a large bowl and stir in the pea shoots until just wilted. Top with the cashew mixture and the crispy shallots.

CHAPTER FOUR

Salads Worthy of a Meal

81-97

Pork Larb *with* Crispy Shallots

I have a real Thai food addiction and it's hard to find here in Hudson, so this recipe is my attempt to satiate my needs, and it works well in a pinch. Ground pork is pan-cooked and then stirred together with a combination of fish sauce, hot chile flakes, shallots, and lime juice, then tossed with green onions and lots of fresh herbs. I also fry up some of the shallots for crunch. If you don't eat pork, ground chicken or turkey (dark meat, please) will work fine in its place. Serve with sticky rice and a cold beer.

SERVES 4

TIME 30 minutes

INGREDIENTS

3 tablespoons jasmine rice

2 large shallots, thinly sliced into rounds

2 tablespoons fish sauce

¼ cup (60 ml) lime juice (from about 2 limes), plus more for serving

½ teaspoon light brown sugar

1 bird's eye chile or serrano pepper, thinly sliced

½ teaspoon red pepper flakes, plus more to taste

3 green onions (both white and green parts), thinly sliced

½ cup (25 g) torn fresh mint leaves

½ cup (20 g) roughly chopped loosely packed fresh cilantro (both leaves and tender stems)

1 tablespoon neutral oil, such as grapeseed or canola

Flaky salt

1 pound (455 g) ground pork

Kosher salt

4 chive blossoms, chopped (optional)

Lime, for serving

METHOD

In a 12-inch (30.5 cm) skillet, toast the rice over medium-high heat until it becomes fragrant and begins to turn golden, 4 to 5 minutes. Transfer to a mortar and pestle or spice grinder and pound or pulse until the rice becomes powder-like (should yield about 1½ tablespoons). Set aside.

In a large bowl, whisk together half the shallots, the fish sauce, lime juice, sugar, bird's eye chile, and red pepper flakes along with half the green onions, half the mint, and half the cilantro until the sugar dissolves, and then set aside.

Wipe out the skillet and heat the grapeseed oil over high heat. Once it shimmers, add the remaining shallots and cook, stirring occasionally, until crispy, 3 to 5 minutes. Place on a paper towel–lined plate and sprinkle with flaky salt.

Wipe out the skillet and heat over medium heat. Add the ground pork, breaking it apart with the back of a spoon, and fry until it is cooked through and no longer pink, 5 to 6 minutes. Remove from heat. Season with salt.

With a slotted spoon, transfer the pork to the herb mixture in the large bowl, along with the rice powder, and stir together until well combined. Season to taste with salt. Top with the remaining green onions, chive blossoms (if using). Finish with the crispy shallots and a good squeeze of lime.

Farro and Pole Bean Salad *with* Almonds & Tarragon

This is a straight-up, versatile grain salad that has lots of possibilities to play with. Try different nut, herb, and citrus combinations such as pistachios, mint, and orange or walnuts, dill, and lime. I like to keep my options open. A crumbly cheese such as feta or ricotta salata would also be a nice addition stirred throughout. You can serve this dish either warm or at room temperature, so feel free to prepare it a few hours in advance if you're trying to get ahead of the game.

SERVES 4 to 6

TIME 35 minutes

INGREDIENTS

1 cup (200 g) farro

Kosher salt

FOR THE GREMOLATA:

½ cup (55 g) chopped almonds

1 cup (50 g) roughly chopped fresh tarragon

2 tablespoons lemon zest

2 tablespoons finely chopped shallot

FOR THE BEANS:

2 tablespoons olive oil

1 pound (455 g) pole or string beans, trimmed

Freshly ground black pepper

Lemon juice or good quality white wine vinegar, such as Katz's Sauvignon Blanc, for finishing

METHOD

In a medium saucepan, bring the farro, 3 cups (720 ml) water, and a pinch of kosher salt to a boil. Turn the heat down to a simmer, cover, and cook until the farro is tender and toothsome, about 25 to 30 minutes.

Meanwhile, make the gremolata: Toast the almonds in a large skillet over medium-low heat, stirring frequently to ensure they don't burn, 4 to 5 minutes. Place in a bowl and stir in the tarragon, lemon zest, and shallots. Season with kosher salt and set aside.

Prepare the beans: Wipe out the skillet and heat the olive oil over medium heat. Add the greens beans and season well with kosher salt and black pepper. Cook, stirring frequently, until the beans are crisp-tender and start to brown in spots, 6 to 8 minutes. Add in a few tablespoons of water to help them along, if needed. Turn off the heat.

If there is any residual cooking liquid from the farro, drain it and add the farro directly to the skillet. Toss with the beans until well combined. Plate in a large bowl or on a platter and top with the gremolata. Squeeze with lemon or drizzle with a bit of the white wine vinegar to finish. Season with salt.

Duck Confit *with* Red Cabbage, Apple, & Caraway Vinaigrette

Don't worry, I'm not asking you to confit your own duck legs. I just happen to get a little slap happy when D'Artagnan has their Black Friday sale and tend to stock up. Duck legs preserved in their own fat elevate any meal, and allow you to casually say when asked what you're serving, "I have some duck confit we can use, *pas de problème!*" One New Year's Eve, I made this dish for a very civilized dinner that started with sliced ham, pâté, fondue, and Champagne, and as you've probably guessed, didn't end quite as refined as it had started. The tartness of the apple and sherry vinaigrette add just the right amount of punch to cut through the richness of the duck. I'd also serve some creamy white beans alongside, and while I think the ham can sit this one out, the Champagne surely shouldn't.

SERVES 4

TIME 30 minutes

INGREDIENTS

4 prepared confit duck legs, at room temperature

FOR THE SALAD:

1 teaspoon caraway seeds, toasted

1½ teaspoons Dijon mustard, preferably the Maille brand

2 tablespoons sherry vinegar

¼ teaspoon honey

5 tablespoons (75 ml) olive oil

Kosher salt and freshly ground black pepper

5 cups (475 g) shredded red cabbage

1 medium tart, crisp apple, such as a Pink Lady or Honeycrisp, cored and thinly sliced

3 scallions (both white and green parts), thinly sliced (about ⅓ cup/35 g)

METHOD

Preheat the oven to 400°F (205°C). In a medium ovenproof or cast-iron skillet, place the legs skin side down snugly in the pan. Heat until the skin is crisp and golden and the meat is warmed through, 25 to 30 minutes total. I've found you do not need to flip the meat.

While the duck warms, prepare your salad: In a medium bowl, whisk together the caraway seeds, mustard, vinegar, and honey. Slowly whisk in the olive oil in a thin stream to emulsify the vinaigrette. Season with salt and pepper.

In a large bowl, gently toss together the cabbage, apple, and green onions and then toss with as much or as little of the vinaigrette as you like. I like to use it all. Taste and adjust seasonings accordingly with salt and pepper. Divide among 4 plates.

Remove the duck legs from the oven and place one over each portion of the salad. Be sure to store whatever duck fat has rendered in the pan in an airtight container. Store in the refrigerator to fry or roast with potatoes at a later date.

A NOTE: *If you do want to make your own duck confit, by all means be a hero. It's not that hard! Carla Lalli Music has a foolproof recipe in her book* Where Cooking Begins *that is worth seeking out.*

Rice Salad *for* a Screened-In Porch Dinner

Growing up in the suburbs of New York City meant screened-in porches for summer dinners. I still have a very strong affection for them. After dinner on the weekends, my no-longer-married parents used to play bridge with their visiting city friends and drink white wine spritzers and snack on in-shell salted peanuts late into the night. This was the mid-eighties after all. I stayed up late too, trying to learn how to cut and riffle cards, always waiting to see who would end up the "dummy," and hoping they might provide me with some entertainment as they had to sit out the round. I affectionately remember many meals spent on the porch off the back of my childhood home and the joyful snap of the screen door closing. I also remember that on sweltery days we'd often have rice salad for dinner. My mom's recipe had salty chunks of provolone, thickly sliced garden tomatoes, and ribbons of romaine, among many other things, which was lovely and, not surprisingly, leaned toward her Italian-American upbringing. I've tried here to recreate something of the like by memory, but to also make it my own. Serve it solo or as a side with grilled fish, spritzer on ice in hand, sweaty brow not required, but likely present.

SERVES 6

TIME 30 minutes

INGREDIENTS

1½ cups (275 g) long-grain white rice

3 ounces (85 g) hard Italian salami, from brands such as La Quercia or Olympia Provisions, cut into ½-inch (12 mm) dice

1 cup (113 g) loosely packed shaved provolone (I like to use a Y-peeler for this.)

2 thinly sliced green onions (both white and green parts)

2 tablespoons capers, rinsed well if in salt

3 cups (45 g) loosely packed baby arugula

1½ cups (120 g) roughly chopped mixed fresh herbs, such as basil and flat-leaf parsley

1 tablespoon olive oil, plus more to taste

3 teaspoons good-quality balsamic vinegar, plus more to taste

METHOD

Bring a large pot of well-salted water to a boil. Add the rice and cook until al dente, about 15 minutes.

Drain and spread in an even layer on a large rimmed baking sheet and let cool for 10 to 15 minutes.

In a large mixing bowl, toss together the rice, salami, provolone, green onions, capers, arugula, and half the herbs.

Drizzle with the olive oil and the vinegar and toss to combine. Drizzling with more of each if desired. Top with the remaining herbs and serve.

Pretending I'm Vacationing *in* Italy Salad

As I write this, I am desperate to be anywhere but here in the Hudson Valley. My wanderlust has peaked, and in my mind I'm in Italy with friends in a big house by the sea. It's July. We likely have just gotten home from the beach and are rummaging through the kitchen to make a late lunch. I find some cucumbers and some local mozzarella and begin to assemble a salad so simple, it deserves the very best of ingredients. I place it on the table with some thickly cut pieces of toasted bread rubbed with garlic and perhaps a plate of sliced, still-warm-from-the-sun tomatoes, and figs too. We sit outside and drink fizzy wine and afternoon slips into evening and we laugh a lot. I'm hoping maybe we'll be together there next summer. For now, I'll make the salad and eat it barefoot on my front porch.

SERVES 4

TIME 10 minutes

INGREDIENTS

2 pounds (910 g) heirloom cucumbers, sliced into ¼-inch-thick rounds

8 ounces (225 g) fresh mozzarella, at room temperature, torn into bite-size pieces

Kosher salt

4 ounces (115 g) prosciutto, torn into bite-size pieces

1 cup (80 g) loosely packed fresh basil leaves (torn if large)

1 teaspoon fresh marjoram leaves (optional)

Good-quality olive oil, for drizzling

Freshly ground black pepper and flaky salt

METHOD

On a medium platter, arrange the cucumbers and mozzarella and season with salt.

Gently and evenly add the prosciutto and top the salad with basil and marjoram, if using.

Drizzle a generous amount of olive oil over everything. Season with a few good turns of black pepper and a few pinches of flaky salt and serve.

Skillet Caesar *with* Charred Lemon and Toasted Garlic

Charring lettuce in a hot pan until it's infused with anchovies, garlic, and olive oil not only gives it beautiful color and texture, but it also tastes pretty great. Toasted garlic and breadcrumbs for crunch also don't hurt. There is no egg component in this version, but if you're feeling adventurous, you could fry or poach one and serve it on top. But in my opinion simplicity is key.

SERVES 4

TIME 25 minutes

INGREDIENTS

4 tablespoons (60 ml) olive oil

2 cups (150 g) torn 1-inch (2.5 cm) pieces of country bread (I like to use a sesame loaf—crust on!)

2 cloves garlic, thinly sliced

4 oil-packed anchovies

3 baby romaine hearts, halved lengthwise

½ lemon

Freshly grated Parmesan cheese, for serving

Flaky salt, for serving

Freshly ground black pepper

METHOD

In a 12-inch (30.5 cm) skillet, heat 2 tablespoons of the oil over medium heat. When it shimmers, add the bread and toast it, stirring occasionally, until golden, 4 to 6 minutes. Remove from the pan and set aside.

If needed, wipe out the skillet and then heat the remaining 2 tablespoons of oil over medium heat. Add the garlic and the anchovies and cook until the anchovies dissolve in the oil and the garlic becomes golden, 2 to 3 minutes. Using a slotted spoon, remove and reserve the garlic.

Add the romaine and the lemon to the pan cut side down in one snug layer. Cook until the lettuce begins to turn brown and golden in spots, 4 to 6 minutes. Flip the romaine and cook for 1 to 2 minutes more.

Arrange the lettuce on a large plate or platter cut side up and squeeze the lemon over the top. Scatter with the reserved garlic and the breadcrumbs and shave Parmesan over the top. Season with flaky salt and a few good turns of black pepper.

A Summer Corn Salad
with Shrimp

Nothing says summer like fresh corn from a farm stand, and there are plenty of those in the Hudson Valley. As a child, when tasked, I'd sit on the back steps of the house and, with pleasure and purpose, tear away the corn husks and brush off their silks. These days, I love sitting outside shucking corn with friends while drinking big tumblers of rosé. This salad was built on a clean-out-the-fridge night and I'm so glad it came to be. Normally I'm not one for green peppers (unless they are the very hot variety), but for some reason I make an expectation for the Italian frying kind, which I use here. Shrimp pairs beautifully with corn, so I said what the heck. As I hope you're making this in the hotter months, it is topped with a generous amount of basil, because that's what summer requires. Serve warm or at room temperature.

SERVES 4

TIME 40 minutes

INGREDIENTS

1 pound (455 g) jumbo shrimp, peeled and deveined, tails removed if you like

Kosher salt and freshly ground black pepper

¼ cup (½ stick/55 g) unsalted butter, cut into tablespoons

1 medium poblano pepper, diced

1 Italian green frying pepper, diced

⅓ cup (35 g) thinly sliced green onions, whites only (from about 3 large scallions)

4 ears corn, husks and silk removed, kernels cut off the cob

8 ounces (225 g) zucchini, finely diced (about 2 cups)

4 ounces (115 g) feta cheese, crumbled

⅓ cup (15 g) loosely packed fresh basil leaves (torn if large)

Lime, for finishing

Flaky salt, for finishing

METHOD

Season the shrimp well with salt and pepper. In a 12-inch (30.5 cm) skillet, heat the butter over medium. Add the shrimp and heat until just cooked through, 1 to 2 minutes per side. Transfer to a medium bowl and set aside.

Add the peppers and the green onions to the skillet and cook, stirring occasionally, until softened, 2 to 3 minutes.

Add the corn and the zucchini and cook, stirring frequently, until they begin to turn golden in spots, 5 to 7 minutes more. Season well with salt and pepper.

Transfer the corn mixture to a large bowl.

Stir in the shrimp, feta cheese, half the basil, and a good squeeze of lime. Taste and adjust seasonings. Top with remaining basil and flaky salt.

Chicories *with* Tuna, Fennel, and Old-School Italian Dressing

I love this salad! It features the classic Italian combination of creamy white beans and oil-packed tuna, and it is tossed with a dressing that will remind you of your childhood, but also with radicchio, which will remind you that you're an adult and like bitter greens. Thinly sliced fennel would also be a nice addition should you have some around. Macerating the shallot in some vinegar for a few minutes takes off the edge and provides pleasant acidity.

SERVES 4 to 6

TIME 15 minutes

INGREDIENTS

FOR THE DRESSING:

½ cup (120 ml) olive oil

5 tablespoons (75 ml) red wine vinegar, plus a bit more for the shallots

1 teaspoon light brown sugar

1 teaspoon dried oregano

1 clove garlic, grated

Kosher salt and freshly ground black pepper

FOR THE SALAD:

1 medium shallot, thinly sliced into rings

Red wine vinegar, for drizzling

Kosher salt

2 jars (6.7-ounce/190 g) oil-packed tuna or good-quality canned tuna, broken into large pieces (I like the Tonnino brand.)

3½ cups (233 g) cooked white beans, such as cannellini or butter beans, or 2 cans (15 ounces/430 g each), drained

Good-quality olive oil, for drizzling

Freshly ground black pepper

1 medium head radicchio, cored, leaves coarsely torn

¼ cup (13 g) roughly chopped flat-leaf parsley (both leaves and tender stems)

Flaky salt, for finishing

Toasted bread, for serving (optional)

METHOD

Make the dressing: Whisk the oil, vinegar, sugar, oregano, and garlic in a small bowl. Season with kosher salt and black pepper and set aside.

Prepare the salad: Place the shallots in a small bowl and pour in just enough vinegar to cover them. Add a pinch of kosher salt and let sit for 5 minutes. Drain and discard the vinegar.

In a medium bowl, gently toss together the shallots, tuna, and white beans, drizzle with a bit of olive oil.

Place the radicchio in a large bowl and toss with a bit of the vinaigrette. Season with salt and pepper and transfer to a large platter.

Arrange the tuna–bean mixture on top and drizzle some more of the vinaigrette. Scatter with parsley and season with flaky salt.

Broiled Mussels with Panko and Pecorino, page 103.

CHAPTER FIVE

Seven *Fish*, No Feast

99-115

Almost Scallop Chowder

One evening I was home alone, puttering about my kitchen as I usually do when left to my own devices, and I was craving something like a chowder, but not quite as hearty as they tend to be. I wanted something brothier and lighter and didn't want to sacrifice the texture of a well-seared scallop, because why would you? I began rifling through my fridge and found a bit of bacon, some leeks, a few celery stalks and some fennel and knew my vision was possible. With the help of some scallops I had purchased earlier in the week, I began to build out my plan. I like making this dish when summer days are growing shorter and the nights are starting to get cool, as it's still possible to get a hold of some farmstand corn. But make it any time of year you'd like.

SERVES 4

TIME 45 minutes

INGREDIENTS

1 tablespoon olive oil

4 ounces (115 g) bacon, finely diced (from about 3 slices)

1 stalk celery, cut into ½-inch (12 mm) pieces

2 medium leeks, thinly sliced crosswise

1 medium fennel bulb, thinly sliced crosswise

1 cup (175 g) corn kernels

Kosher salt and freshly ground black pepper

3 sprigs thyme

1 pound (455 g) small red or yellow potatoes, thinly sliced into ¼-inch rounds

3 to 3½ cups (720 to 840 ml) chicken stock

16 scallops (about 1 pound/448 g), patted very dry

2 tablespoons grapeseed or canola oil

½ cup (120 ml) heavy cream

¼ cup (7.5 g) roughly chopped celery leaves

½ cup (20 g) loosely packed torn fresh basil leaves

Flaky salt, for finishing (optional)

METHOD

In a deep 12-inch (30.5 cm) skillet, heat the oil over medium heat. Add the bacon and cook, stirring occasionally, until crispy, 5 to 7 minutes. Set aside on a paper towel–lined plate.

Add the celery, leeks, fennel, and corn to the pan and season with salt and pepper. Cook, stirring frequently, until the vegetables are softened and the corn begins to take on a bit of golden color, 3 to 5 minutes.

Stir in the thyme and the potatoes and toss with the other vegetables until coated with bacon fat. Pour in enough chicken stock to make sure all the potatoes are submerged in liquid. (Give it a quick stir to check.) Bring to a simmer and cook until the potatoes are soft, but still maintain their structure, 10 to 15 minutes.

(Continued)

While the potatoes cook, make your scallops. Season the scallops well with salt. Heat a 12-inch (30.5 cm) nonstick skillet or well-seasoned cast-iron pan over high heat until just about smoking, 2 to 3 minutes. Add the oil and when it shimmers, add the scallops (working in batches to avoid crowding the pan, if needed) and cook until golden brown and crisp, flipping once, 1 to 2 minutes per side. Remove from the pan and set aside on a paper-towel lined plate.

When the potatoes are finished cooking, add the bacon back to the pan, turn off the heat, and pour in the cream, stirring until it is warmed through. Remove and discard the thyme stems.

Ladle the broth and potato mixture into bowls and top each serving with 3 or 4 scallops. Scatter the celery leaves and basil over each portion and season with flaky salt if you like.

A NOTE: *If you'd like to make this dish, but scallops aren't available, shrimp is a fine substitution. You can brown the shrimp and set them aside or simply add them into the broth to poach for 2 to 3 minutes before serving, then stir in the cream.*

Broiled Mussels *with* Panko and Pecorino

These mussels are one of the first recipes I created when I really got into cooking in my early twenties. They are also the first menu item that I was able to incorporate into my family's (pretty extensive) Feast of the Seven Fishes menu and, boy, was I proud. They are a take on another one of my favorite dishes, baked clams. I am stuffing shellfish with a mixture that incorporates grated pecorino cheese. I am pleased with breaking this so-called taboo. These could be served as part of a cocktail party menu, but when accompanied with a bright salad of bitter greens they make for a lovely, light supper.

SERVES 4, as a snack

TIME 25 minutes

INGREDIENTS

¾ cup (72 g) panko

2 cloves garlic, grated

½ cup (65 g) freshly grated pecorino cheese

2 tablespoons finely chopped fresh flat-leaf parsley

2 teaspoons lemon zest

¼ cup (60 ml) olive oil, plus more for drizzling

Kosher salt and freshly ground black pepper

½ cup (120 ml) white wine

2 pounds (910 g) mussels, scrubbed and debearded

METHOD

Put the panko, garlic, cheese, parsley, and lemon zest in a medium bowl and mix to combine. Add the olive oil and stir until the breadcrumbs are well coated in the oil. Season to taste with kosher salt and black pepper and set the filling aside.

Pour the wine into a large Dutch oven and bring to a steady simmer over medium heat. Add the mussels and cover. Cook until the mussels have steamed open, 3 to 4 minutes, and place them in a large bowl. Discard the cooking liquid.

When cool enough to touch, snap off each shell that is not cradling a mussel and discard it. Place the mussels in their shells on a large rimmed baking sheet and, using a small spoon, top each mussel with some of the filling. Drizzle each one with a bit more olive oil.

Preheat the oven to broil and cook the mussels until the breadcrumbs are golden and crispy, rotating the pan halfway through if needed for even cooking and checking frequently to make sure they don't burn (every broiler is different), 2 to 3 minutes. Serve on a plate or platter.

Swordfish *with* Burst Tomatoes, Peppers, and Za'atar and Preserved Lemon

My dad ordered swordfish a lot when we vacationed on the Cape in the eighties. He also spent a lot of time unsuccessfully surf casting on Nauset Beach, but that's another story. In the years following, swordfish became so overfished that for many years it was taken off menus. Since then, a lot of work has been done to rebuild the population and I'm so pleased we're able to eat them responsibly again. They are meaty, flavorful, wonderful fish that hold their own with punchy flavors, which you'll see here. If you can find the Italian Jimmy Nardello varietal of peppers for this recipe, please do. They are up there as one of my favorite peppers, and when cooked, their sweetness intensifies and almost becomes a bit smoky. I first had them in Napa and was thrilled when the farmers at Sparrowbush started growing them here in Hudson. Clearly a bell pepper will also work, but I think the Nardello's are worth tracking down.

SERVES 4

TIME 35 minutes

INGREDIENTS

4 tablespoons (60 ml) olive oil

3 Jimmy Nardello peppers or 1 medium red bell pepper, seeded and cut into long thin strips

2 pints (290 g) mixed heirloom cherry tomatoes, halved if large

2 cloves garlic, thinly sliced

1 chile pepper, such as cayenne, serrano, or jalapeño, thinly sliced

2½ teaspoons za'atar (a Middle Eastern spice blend consisting of dried herbs and sesame seeds)

¼ cup (112 g) seeded and roughly chopped preserved lemon (both peel and flesh)

½ cup (120 ml) dry white wine

Kosher salt and freshly ground black pepper

4 (6-ounce/170 g) swordfish steaks, about ¾ inch (2 cm) thick

2 tablespoons fresh oregano leaves

Flaky salt, for finishing (optional)

(Continued)

METHOD

Heat 2 tablespoons of the oil in a deep-sided 12-inch (30.5 cm) skillet over medium heat. Add the sweet peppers and cook, stirring occasionally, until they are softened and beginning to turn golden in spots, 6 to 8 minutes.

Add the cherry tomatoes to the skillet and cook, stirring occasionally, until they start to burst, 5 to 7 minutes, pressing the tomatoes gently with the back of a spatula or wooden spoon to get them nice and jammy. (I like to keep some with more structure than the others for texture's sake.) There should be a fair amount of liquid released in the pan. If not, add a few tablespoons of water.

Stir in the garlic, chile pepper, za'atar, and preserved lemon and cook for 2 to 3 minutes more, until the garlic is fragrant and the spice mix is lightly toasted.

Pour in the white wine and bring to a simmer, scraping up any brown bits that have formed at the bottom of the pan, and cook for 10 minutes or so, allowing the flavors to get to know each other and the sauce to slightly thicken. Taste and adjust with salt and pepper.

Meanwhile, prepare the swordfish steaks. Season the fish well with salt and pepper. Heat the remaining 2 tablespoons of oil in a large nonstick skillet over medium-high heat. Add the fish and cook for 3 to 4 minutes, and then gently flip to finish cooking, 2 to 3 minutes more, or until the flesh is opaque all the way through. Arrange the swordfish in the pan with the tomatoes and peppers and scatter the top with the oregano leaves. Season with flaky salt if you like. Spoon more of the sauce over the top and serve from the pan.

Cumin, Ginger, and Citrus Roasted Salmon *with* Cabbage, Dates, and Creamy Tahini Dressing

I lost around thirty pounds between the fall of 2018 and summer of 2019. They were pounds I needed to lose for my health. During that time I also ate a lot of salmon. In the past, I never sought out salmon, I never craved salmon, and it wasn't something I grew up with at the table, but during my year and a half journey (read: ongoing), salmon suddenly and happily became a regular part of my diet. It cooks quickly, is filling, takes on whatever flavors you assign it, and it feels luxurious to eat! Kind of a no-brainer. This dinner comes with a tahini and lime tossed salad of cabbage, dates, and almonds—no need to ask for dressing on the side.

SERVES 4

TIME 30 minutes

INGREDIENTS

FOR THE SALMON:

4 (6-ounce/170 g) salmon fillets, preferably center cut, 1 to 1½ inches (2.5 to 4 cm) thick

Kosher salt and freshly ground black pepper

2 teaspoons ground cumin

2 teaspoons grated fresh ginger

1 clove garlic, grated

2 teaspoons olive oil

2 teaspoons orange zest

¼ cup (60 ml) freshly squeezed orange juice

FOR THE SIDE SALAD:

2 tablespoons warm water, plus more as needed

2 tablespoons tahini

2 tablespoons fresh lime juice

1 teaspoon honey

Kosher salt and freshly ground black pepper

5 cups (475 g) thinly sliced savoy or napa cabbage

8 Medjool dates, roughly chopped

¼ cup (30 g) chopped almonds

1 cup (40 g) roughly chopped loosely packed fresh cilantro (both leaves and tender stems)

Olive oil, for drizzling

Flaky salt, for serving

(Continued)

METHOD

Preheat the oven to 450°F (230°C) and line a sheet pan with parchment.

While the oven heats, prep the salmon: Season the fillets well with salt and black pepper and place them in a shallow bowl or plate. In a small bowl, whisk together the cumin, ginger, garlic, olive oil, orange zest, and juice and season with salt and pepper. Pour the dressing over the top of the salmon and rub it all over the sides of the fish. Set aside to marinate while you make your side salad.

In a medium bowl, whisk together the warm water, tahini, lime juice, and honey and season with salt and black pepper. If needed, whisk in a few more tablespoons of warm water to loosen it up a bit.

In a large skillet, toast the almonds over medium-low heat, stirring frequently so they do not burn, 4 to 5 minutes.

In a large bowl, toss together the cabbage, dates, almonds, and cilantro and season well with salt and black pepper. Pour in the salad dressing and toss again to make sure everything is well coated. Drizzle with olive oil. Taste and adjust seasoning.

Roast the salmon in the preheated oven until the fillets are just cooked through, 10 to 12 minutes. (See "A Note" below.)

Serve the salmon on top of the cabbage salad or alongside. Finish with flaky salt.

A NOTE: *If you like your salmon to be a bit more golden (I do), pop it under the broiler for a minute or so, watching it carefully to make sure it doesn't overcook or burn.*

Smoky and Spicy Shrimp *with* Anchovy Butter and Fregola

It's all right there for you in the title. Sweet shrimp is sautéed until just cooked through, and fregola (a tiny toasted pasta from Sardinia) is added to the pot to toast in the melted anchovy butter and spices with some cherry tomatoes. I love Calabrian chiles packed in oil and use them here for some punchy heat, but if red pepper flakes are within closer reach feel free to use them instead. Once the fregola finishes cooking, return the shrimp to the pot to warm them through and serve straight from the pan. Serve with many bottles of chilled red wine.

SERVES 4

TIME 30 minutes

INGREDIENTS

1 pound (455 g) extra-large or jumbo shrimp, peeled and deveined

Kosher salt and freshly ground black pepper

¼ cup (½ stick/55 g) unsalted butter

4 cloves garlic, thinly sliced

4 oil-packed anchovies

3 Calabrian chiles, roughly chopped, or 1 teaspoon red pepper flakes

½ teaspoon smoked paprika

2 tablespoons tomato paste

1 pint (290 g) cherry or Sungold tomatoes

1½ cups (270 g) fregola

3 cups (700 ml) chicken stock

½ cup (20 g) loosely packed basil leaves, torn if large, or roughly chopped parsley or mint, or a combination of all three

METHOD

Season the shrimp well with salt and black pepper. In a 12-inch (30.5 cm) skillet, melt the butter over medium heat. Add the shrimp and cook until pink, 1 to 2 minutes per side. Remove and set aside on a plate.

Add the garlic, anchovies, Calabrian chiles, and smoked paprika to the skillet and stir until the garlic is fragrant and the anchovies have dissolved, about 2 minutes.

Add the tomato paste and toast for a minute or so. Add the cherry tomatoes and stir to coat. Cook until the tomatoes begin to burst, pressing down on them gently to help release their liquid, 3 to 4 minutes.

Add the fregola to the pan and stir until the pasta is well coated in the spiced butter. Pour in the stock and bring to a boil. Reduce the heat to low, cover, and simmer until the fregola is al dente, 10 to 12 minutes.

Add the shrimp back to the pan with any juices that have accumulated on the plate and stir until they are just warmed through. Scatter with herbs and serve.

Crispy Fish *with* Quick Tomatillo and Jalapeño Confit

I made this for my friend Alexis one Monday night and she declared it "the best!" I don't know if my self-deprecating self would go that far, but it is very good. Tangy tomatillos are slowly cooked down in olive oil with some jalapeños and a bit of brown sugar for a playful take on a quick confit and spooned on top of the fish right before serving. You don't need to flour the fish to get a crispy crust, just make sure you heat your pan very well before you add the oil to ensure you do. If it's not a crispy fish night, feel free to make the confit anyway; you can spoon it on top of grilled shrimp or other fish, roast chicken, beef, or pork.

SERVES 4

TIME 30 minutes

INGREDIENTS

1 pound (455 g) tomatillos, husked, rinsed, and halved or quartered if large

2 jalapeños, thinly sliced into rings, seeds removed if you like

3 green onions, cut into ½-inch (12 mm) pieces, whites and dark green parts kept separate

½ teaspoon light brown sugar, plus more to taste

Kosher salt

1 cup (240 ml) olive oil

4 (6-ounce/168 g) skin-on red snapper or black bass fillets

2 tablespoons grapeseed or canola oil

Flaky salt, for finishing

METHOD

In a medium saucepan, put the tomatillos, jalapeños, white parts of green onions, and light brown sugar and season with salt. Cover the vegetables with the olive oil and bring to a low simmer over medium-low heat. Cook, stirring occasionally, until the tomatillos have softened, pressing down on some so they break down, 15 to 20 minutes. Taste and adjust the seasonings with salt and brown sugar to taste. Keep at a low simmer while you cook the fish.

Season the fish well with salt. Heat a 12-inch (30.5 cm) nonstick skillet or well-seasoned cast-iron pan over high heat for 2 to 3 minutes. You want the pan very hot to crisp the fish. Add the grapeseed oil and when it shimmers, add the fillets skin side down in the pan. Immediately press the fish down with a fish spatula so as much skin as possible has contact with the pan and cook until the flesh is beginning to turn opaque and the skin is very crispy, 2 to 3 minutes. Flip and cook 1 to 2 minutes more on the other side.

Plate the fish and spoon some of the tomatillo–jalapeño confit on top. Scatter with the reserved green parts of the green onions and season with flaky salt. Pass the remaining sauce at the table.

Seafood Stew *with* Toasted Coriander and Harissa

This stew is on the brothier end of the spectrum. I used spicy harissa paste and chopped tomato along with fennel and toasted coriander as the stew's base, but tomato paste and some chile flakes could also work if they're easier to find than harissa. I think three types of fish provide enough variety, but you could add or swap in mussels or squid should you like. As you will learn, clams (for me) are not optional.

SERVES 4

TIME 30 minutes

INGREDIENTS

2 tablespoons olive oil

1 large shallot, thinly sliced

1 medium fennel bulb, thinly sliced

3 tablespoons harissa paste (I like the hot version, but the choice is up to you.)

1½ teaspoons crushed coriander seeds

1 medium tomato, seeded and coarsely chopped

3 cloves garlic, finely chopped

Kosher salt

1 cup (240 ml) white wine or dry vermouth

2 cups (480 ml) fish or vegetable stock

1 dozen littleneck clams

1¼ pounds (570 g) halibut or cod, cut into 1-inch (2.5 cm) pieces

12 ounces (340 g) jumbo shrimp, peeled and deveined

¼ cup (56.7 g) roughly chopped fresh cilantro and dill, for serving

Olive oil–toasted bread rubbed with garlic, for serving

METHOD

In a large Dutch oven or stockpot, heat the oil over medium heat. When it shimmers, add the shallot and fennel and cook until softened, 3 to 5 minutes. Stir in the harissa and crushed coriander and cook until they have toasted slightly, 3 minutes or so. Add in the tomato and garlic and cook for 1 minute more. Season with salt.

Add the wine to the pot and cook until the liquid is reduced by half, 5 to 7 minutes. Pour in the fish stock and bring to a simmer.

Add the clams, cover, and cook until most of them begin to pop open, 3 to 5 minutes. Add the halibut and shrimp, cover, and simmer until they are cooked through and the remaining clams have opened, 2 to 3 minutes more.

Using a slotted spoon, divide the seafood among four bowls. Ladle the broth into the bowls and top each portion with a bit of cilantro and dill. Serve with olive oil–toasted bread rubbed with garlic.

CHAPTER SIX

When in Need *of* Comfort

117-155

A Pot *of* Beans

I have made beans on a weekly basis for years (mostly on Sundays), so I can use them in meals throughout the week. They are dependable, comforting, and delicious. Not only do they have the ability to serve as a satisfying, delightful meal on their own, they also offer you the flexibility of using them to transform an already existing dish. There isn't much a bean can't do.

SERVES Many

TIME Truly depends on the bean, likely about an hour or so, if soaked beforehand

INGREDIENTS

1 pound (455 g) dried beans

1 tablespoon kosher salt

1 large yellow onion, peeled and halved, or some leek tops, or a few peeled and halved shallots

1 celery stalk with its leaves, cut in half

6 cloves garlic, smashed with the back of a knife, skins discarded

Thyme, rosemary, and parsley sprigs, tied in a bundle with kitchen twine (optional)

Olive oil

METHOD

In a large Dutch oven or stockpot, add the beans and the salt and cover them by about 2 inches (5 cm) of water and soak overnight or 6 to 8 hours.

When you're ready to cook the beans, do not drain them. Add the onion, celery, garlic, and herbs (if using) to the pot of beans. Add more water if needed to make sure the beans are still covered by about 2 inches (5 cm) and drizzle with a good glug or two of olive oil.

Bring the pot of beans to a boil and then turn down the heat to barely a simmer. Skim off any grit and cook until the beans are creamy and tender, adding boiling water along the way, if needed, to make sure your beans stay submerged. This can take anywhere from 1 to 2 hours. Taste your beans along the way; some types of beans will take longer than others. When they are creamy and make you sigh with joy when you bite into a small handful, they are done.

Remove the aromatics, salt to taste, and serve. To store, let cool and then refrigerate them in their broth for up to 1 week or freeze them for up to 6 months.

(Continued)

MAKE IT A MEAL

Weekday Cassoulet: Preheat the oven to 400°F (205°C). Brown some well-seasoned chicken thighs in canola oil over medium-high heat, then brown a few sausages and set aside. Turn the heat down to medium and sauté finely chopped onion, celery, and garlic. If you have it, adding in a few teaspoons of fresh thyme or rosemary would be nice too. Stir in a handful of crushed tomatoes and some white beans and season with salt and pepper. Transfer the mixture to a 9 by 13-inch (23 by 33 cm) pan and nestle the chicken and sausage in the beans. Bake until the chicken is almost cooked through, 15 to 20 minutes. Top with fresh, coarse breadcrumbs and drizzle with plenty of olive oil. Broil until the top is crispy and golden, a few minutes more.

Tomato Confit and White Bean Stew: Sauté a thinly sliced onion, some garlic, and a pinch of red pepper flakes in a good glug of olive oil over medium heat. Add in 4 cups (680 g) beans and about 1 cup (240 ml) of their cooking liquid; smash ½ cup (85 g) or so of the beans to release some of their creaminess. Season with salt and freshly ground black pepper. Stir in 2 to 3 cups (300 to 450 g) tomato confit (page 55) or other roasted or canned cherry tomatoes and simmer for 5 to 10 minutes. Taste and adjust seasonings accordingly. Ladle into bowls and shower with a handful of roughly chopped fresh flat-leaf parsley, lemon zest, some grated pecorino cheese, and a drizzle of olive oil.

Pasta e Fagioli Another Way: Toss 2½ to 3 cups (425 to 510 g) borlotti beans with some mezze rigatoni along with some of the bean cooking water to get it nice and saucy. Drizzle with plenty of olive oil and copious amounts of grated pecorino cheese and top with roughly chopped fresh flat-leaf parsley and basil.

Skillet Pork Chops *with* Vinegar and Honey Collards

There is something undeniably nostalgic to me about cutting into a pork chop. When I was growing up, we ate boneless ones quickly fried in olive oil frequently, alongside baked potatoes slathered in salted butter and topped with sour cream. I've chosen bone-in pork rib chops for richer flavor, plus they have a tasty fat cap to gnaw on post meal. The chops are pan-seared to give them a good crust and set aside to rest while the collard greens are cooked down in the residual pork fat and quickly braised in a mixture of tangy vinegar and a bit of honey. Feel free to use kale in place of collards if it is easier to find. Serve with potatoes however you like them best served.

SERVES 4

TIME 30 minutes

INGREDIENTS

½ cup (120 ml) warm water

½ cup (120 ml) good-quality cider vinegar

2 teaspoons honey

4 bone-in pork rib chops, 1 inch (2.5 cm) thick

Kosher salt and freshly ground black pepper

2 tablespoons canola or grapeseed oil

4 cloves garlic, smashed and peeled

½ teaspoon red pepper flakes

1 large yellow onion, halved and thinly sliced

2 bunches collard greens, tough stems and center ribs discarded, cut into 1-inch-wide (2.5 cm) ribbons

Flaky salt, for serving

METHOD

Whisk together the warm water, vinegar, and honey until the honey dissolves. Set aside.

Season the pork chops well with salt and black pepper. If you can do this the evening before and let them sit uncovered overnight, you've planned well; if not, allow them to sit at room temperature for about 30 minutes.

Heat a large cast-iron pan over medium-high heat until very hot, 2 to 3 minutes. Add the oil and when it shimmers, add the pork chops, working in batches if needed to avoid crowding the pan. Cook undisturbed, including the fat caps, until a golden brown crust appears and the pork chops are cooked through, 3 to 4 minutes per side. Transfer to a plate and allow them to rest.

(Continued)

Turn the heat to medium-low and add the garlic, red pepper flakes, and onion to the pan. Cook, stirring frequently, until the onion begins to soften and starts to crisp around some of the edges, about 3 minutes. Add in the collard greens and toss frequently until they begin to wilt, about 5 minutes more.

Stir the vinegar-honey mixture into the skillet and scrape up any brown bits that have formed at the bottom of the pan. Cook until the liquid has been reduced by half, 2 to 3 minutes. Season with kosher salt and black pepper and remove from heat.

Slice the pork chops or keep them whole and serve on top of the greens in the pan. Season everything with flaky salt.

A NOTE: *You should really make baked potatoes to serve alongside. Preheat the oven to 450°F (230°C). With a fork, poke some holes into the potatoes on all sides; I usually do 8 to 10 pricks depending on the size. Place the potatoes directly on the oven rack and roast for about an hour. Serve with plenty of salted butter and sour cream.*

Soupy Beans *with* 'Nduja and Torn Radicchio

Yes, we know this recipe can't be bad because 'nduja is involved—so it's almost not even fair. But, while on the one hand I'm giving you a cheat ingredient that makes everything taste better, on the other, I'm asking you very kindly to make your beans from scratch (page 118) and not use canned ones. The bean water used in this recipe is integral to making its soupiness do its thing. Plus, I imagine by this point in the book you too are making beans on Sundays, so you're probably already ahead of the game? If not, please start soaking right now! I promise you'll thank me.

SERVES 4

TIME 10 minutes, plus bean soaking and cooking time

INGREDIENTS

1 tablespoon olive oil, plus more for drizzling

4 ounces (115 g) 'nduja (a spicy, spreadable sausage from Calabria)

4 cups (740 g) cooked large white or black beans, such as Corona, Scarlett Runner, or butter beans, 1 to 1½ cups (360 to 480 ml) cooking water reserved

2 medium heads (about 10 ounces/280 g) Castelfranco (or other readily available) radicchio, leaves separated and torn

½ cup (20 g) torn fresh herbs, such as basil, mint, or flat-leaf parsley

Grated pecorino or Parmesan cheese, for serving (optional)

METHOD

Heat the oil in a 12-inch (30.5 cm) skillet over medium heat. Add the 'nduja and cook until it begins to melt, 2 to 3 minutes.

Add the beans and 1 cup (240 ml) of the reserved cooking liquid and stir until the beans are coated with the 'nduja oil. Allow to simmer for a minute or so, adding in the additional ½ cup (120 ml) cooking liquid if the beans look dry.

Add in the radicchio leaves and toss until they are gently wilted. Ladle the soupy beans into soup bowls and top with the torn herbs. Drizzle with additional olive oil and some grated cheese if you like.

Sausage, Peppers, and Onions *with* Melty Caprese

I love sausage and peppers and I love a caprese salad, so I thought: Why not combine the two, but melt the cheese? I gave myself a real good pat on the back for this one, thank you. Everything is prepared and cooked in the same pan, making this a breeze to assemble and leaving you with only some bread to toast and a bright and bitter salad to toss to round out this one-stop shop.

SERVES 4

TIME 45 minutes

INGREDIENTS

1 pound (455 g) sweet peppers, such as Jimmy Nardello, banana, or bell peppers, or a combination of all three, seeded and cut lengthwise into 2-inch (5 cm) wide pieces

1 medium red onion, cut lengthwise into ½-inch-thick wedges

1 pint (145 g) cherry, grape, or other small tomatoes

2 tablespoons olive oil

Kosher salt and freshly ground black pepper

1 pound (455 g) sweet or spicy Italian sausages

4 ounces (115 g) fresh mozzarella cheese, torn into 1½- to 2-inch (4 to 5 cm) pieces

¼ cup (10 g) roughly torn, loosely packed basil leaves

METHOD

Preheat the oven to 400°F (205°C). In a deep-sided 12-inch (30.5 cm) skillet, toss together the peppers, onions, and tomatoes with the olive oil until well combined and season with salt and pepper. Nestle the sausages on top of the pepper mixture.

Roast until the vegetables begin to get melty and golden brown around the edges and the sausages are cooked through, 35 to 40 minutes, stirring the vegetables and flipping the sausages over halfway through to ensure even browning.

Remove the pan from the oven and evenly distribute the mozzarella on top. Return to the oven until the cheese has melted, 2 to 3 minutes more. Top with the basil and serve in the pan.

Crispy Lamb *with* Cumin, Leeks, and Celery

This is my hot take on cumin lamb inspired by the many Szechuan restaurants I visit as frequently as I can. It's clearly not authentic, but it sure does taste good and works well when I can't pop down to Chinatown in the city for a quick fix. I like taking the leeks and celery to the edge of caramelization, giving them golden crunchy edges, but still keeping some of that celery snap. I serve this dish in leaves of vegetables such as cabbage, raddichio, or butter lettuce for scooping up the crispy meat, and alongside a bowl of steamed rice.

SERVES 4

TIME 30 minutes

INGREDIENTS

2 to 3 tablespoons grapeseed or canola oil

2 medium leeks, white and tender green parts only, thinly sliced

2 ribs celery, sliced ½ inch (12 mm) thick on the bias, plus ¼ cup (7.5 g) roughly chopped celery leaves for garnish

3 cloves garlic, thinly sliced

2 chile peppers, such as cayenne, Fresno, or serrano, thinly sliced

1 tablespoon cumin seeds

Kosher salt

1 pound (455 g) ground lamb

2 tablespoons thinly sliced green onions (green parts only)

¼ cup (10 g) roughly chopped loosely and packed fresh cilantro (both leaves and tender stems)

Lime wedges, for serving

Leaves of cabbage, radicchio, or butter lettuce, for serving

Steamed rice, for serving

METHOD

Heat a 12-inch (30.5 cm) skillet over medium-high heat. Add 2 tablespoons of the oil and when it shimmers, add the leeks, celery, garlic, chiles, and cumin seeds. Season with salt and cook, stirring occasionally, until the leeks have softened and are starting to brown around the edges and the cumin seeds are aromatic, 5 to 7 minutes. Spoon into a large bowl and set aside.

If the pan looks dry, add the additional tablespoon of oil, and then add the lamb to the pan in one even layer. Flatten the meat with the back of a spatula or spoon and cook undisturbed for 5 to 7 minutes, allowing the lamb to get brown and crispy in spots. Season with salt and flip to ensure even browning, about 5 minutes more. Break into bite-size pieces with the spatula.

With a slotted spoon, transfer the lamb to the leek and celery mixture and toss to combine. Taste and adjust seasonings accordingly. Top with the celery leaves, green onions, cilantro, and a squeeze of lime.

Gingery Lamb Meatballs *with* Tomato Confit Broth and Seeded Yogurt

This recipe came about after a tomato confit–making craze one August. Coincidentally, Applestone Meat Co., an amazing butcher automat (yes, you read that right) opened down the street from our house right around that time, giving me easy access to local meat. I have always loved ground lamb. I like mixing it with spices, putting it on top of flatbread, and giving it a quick broil before topping it with herbs. I also love making a meat sauce out of it, but mostly I love it for making meatballs. And yes, while you could fry them in oil, I generally don't love the cleanup part of that process, so I opt for the oven instead. You can flip the meatballs halfway through the cooking time to give them some equal-sided crispiness, but I'm lazy, so I just serve them on the one side that has crisped up all goldeny for presentation's sake. I loosen up some tomato confit with broth to serve them in and I like serving the seeded yogurt alongside.

SERVES 4 to 6

TIME 45 minutes

INGREDIENTS

FOR THE MEATBALLS:

1 pound (455 g) ground lamb

1 clove garlic, grated

1½ teaspoons grated fresh ginger

½ teaspoon ground cumin

Pinch of Aleppo pepper or red pepper flakes

¼ cup (13 g) finely chopped fresh flat-leaf parsley

1 teaspoon kosher salt, plus more for the seasoning

½ cup (50 g) panko

1 large egg

½ cup (120 ml) full-fat Greek yogurt

1 tablespoon fresh lemon juice

2 teaspoons cumin seeds

FOR THE TOMATO CONFIT:

2 cups (300 g) confit-like cherry tomatoes (recipe on page 55)

½ teaspoon cinnamon

1 cup (240 ml) chicken stock, plus ½ to ¾ cup (115 to 175 ml) more if needed

Cooked orzo or pearled couscous, for serving

¼ cup (13 g) roughly chopped fresh dill, mint, or parsley or a combination of all three, for garnish

(Continued)

METHOD

Make the meatballs: Preheat the oven to 425°F (220°C). In a large bowl, combine the lamb, garlic, ginger, cumin, Aleppo pepper, parsley, 1 teaspoon salt, panko, and egg and mix together well with your hands.

With damp hands, roll the lamb mixture into small balls, about 1 inch (2.5 cm) in diameter; it should yield about 25 meatballs. Place the meatballs on a large rimmed baking sheet and bake until they are cooked through and golden brown on the bottom, 9 to 11 minutes.

Meanwhile, stir together the yogurt with the lemon juice and season with salt. Heat a large skillet over medium heat and toast the cumin seeds, stirring often, until they are fragrant, 1 to 2 minutes. Stir the cumin seeds into the yogurt and set aside.

Wipe out the skillet, add the tomato confit and cinnamon to the pan, and bring to a gentle simmer over low heat. Pour in the chicken stock and simmer for 2 to 3 minutes more. When the meatballs are finished cooking, add them to the tomato confit broth, stir to coat them with the sauce, and heat until warmed through, adding ½ to ¾ cup (115 ml to 175 ml) more stock, if needed, to get the brothy consistency of your preference.

Serve the meatballs over orzo or pearled couscous in bowls and spoon the tomato confit broth over the top. Scatter with herbs and pass the yogurt at the table to spoon on top.

A Roasted Squash Soup

There comes a time every winter season when the squash I purchased at the market with good intentions appears to stare back at me challengingly: "When will you finally use me?" So after weeks of staring at it each morning as I reach for my coffee, I finally decide to make this soup. I roast the squash for extra depth of flavor and the harissa paste gives the soup a bit of smoky heat. Coconut milk, ginger, and squash are always a good match so I add some of those in here too. Everything simmers for a little while so old friends can become reacquainted and by the time I'm ladling the fragrant, silky soup into my mug or bowl, I begin to wonder why I don't make it more often.

SERVES 4 to 6

TIME 45 minutes

INGREDIENTS

1 kabocha or large butternut squash (about 3 pounds/1.4 kg), halved and scraped of seeds

3 tablespoons olive oil, plus more for drizzling

Kosher salt and freshly ground black pepper

1 medium yellow onion, finely chopped

1 (3-inch/7.5 cm) piece fresh ginger, peeled and finely chopped

3 cloves garlic, finely chopped

2 tablespoons medium-hot harissa paste

1 can (15 ounces/445 ml) full-fat unsweeted coconut milk

4 cups (960 ml) chicken broth, vegetable broth, or water

Roughly chopped fresh cilantro, thinly sliced green onions, toasted walnuts or squash seeds, and/or full-fat Greek yogurt, for garnishing (optional)

METHOD

Preheat the oven to 425°F (220°C). Place the squash on a large rimmed sheet pan, drizzle with olive oil, and season well with salt and pepper. Roast flesh side up, until the squash can be easily pierced with a fork and the skin is almost collapsing, 35 to 40 minutes. Allow to cool. Scoop the squash into a bowl and discard the skin.

In a stockpot or Dutch oven, heat the 3 tablespoons olive oil over medium heat. Add the onion and ginger and cook until softened, 4 to 5 minutes. Add the garlic and cook for 30 seconds more. Season well with salt.

Stir in the harissa paste and cook until slightly toasted, 1 to 2 minutes. Add in the squash and stir everything to coat in the harissa oil.

Stir in the coconut milk and stock and bring to a simmer. Cook, allowing the flavors to mingle, for 10 to 15 minutes more. Taste and adjust seasonings with salt as needed.

Allow the soup to cool slightly and, using an immersion blender (or in a standing blender in batches), puree the soup until you have achieved the consistency you like. I like mine pretty smooth. Ladle into bowls and garnish as you like.

Ricotta *and* Pecorino Gnocchi

Tamar suggested I put a ricotta gnocchi recipe in the book, one evening over a few glasses of wine. "They couldn't be easier!" she exclaimed as I looked on skeptically, afraid of flour and failure. But in a moment of courage I decide to explore. Tamar and I are both unfussy cooks and if she proclaims something to be effortless, I'm inclined to believe her, and I'm so happy I did. These puffs of egg and cheese are simple, pillowy dreams. Plus they make me feel like a very accomplished cook, which one could ascertain is the reason I love them so much. They are also incredibly versatile—they work well gently tossed in your favorite pasta sauce or soup—and will charm even your most discerning eater. They are also lovely in a quick take on "chicken and dumplings" or stirred into mushrooms and brown butter. I like using the Calabro brand of ricotta for this recipe, which is hand dipped and doesn't need to be drained prior to mixing in order for the dough to come together. But if it's not within reach make sure to drain the cheese for at least 30 minutes ahead of assembly.

SERVES 4

TIME 20 minutes

INGREDIENTS

1 container (15 ounces/430 g) good-quality whole-milk ricotta cheese, such as the Calabro brand, drained if cheese has excess moisture (see Note)

4 ounces (115 g) finely grated pecorino cheese (about 1 cup; I like the pre-grated Locatelli brand.)

1 large egg

1 large egg yolk

1/4 cup (30 g) all-purpose flour, plus more for dusting

Kosher salt and freshly ground black pepper

METHOD

In a large bowl, put the ricotta, pecorino, egg and egg yolk, and the flour. Season well with salt and pepper and gently stir to combine.

Transfer the dough to a lightly floured work surface and gently form into a ball.

With a bench scraper, cut the dough into quarters. Working with one-quarter at a time and using your hands, roll each piece of dough into a log about 6 inches (15 cm) long.

Using the bench scraper, cut each of the logs - into roughly 6 to 8 gnocchi. Transfer to a lightly floured sheet pan or parchment paper and gently toss with a bit more flour to prevent the gnocchi from sticking. Cook in well salted boiling water until they rise to the surface, roughly 30 seconds, and toss gently with sauce.

(Continued)

SOME SERVING SUGGESTIONS

Gnocchi with Mushrooms and Brown Butter:
Heat 2 tablespoons olive oil in a 12-inch (30.5 cm) skillet over medium heat. Add about 1 pound (455 g) mixed mushrooms, which have been torn into bite-size pieces, and season with salt and pepper. Cook until they begin browning and getting crisp at the edges, 12 to 14 minutes. Add in a stick (1/2 cup/115 g) of butter and a finely chopped shallot. Cook until the butter melts and starts to become nutty. Ladle in some of the pasta cooking water and simmer until the sauce begins to thicken. Add the gnocchi and gently toss to coat in the sauce. Serve in bowls topped with finely chopped fresh parsley and lemon zest.

Gnocchi Tossed in Simple Tomato Sauce:
Heat 2 tablespoons olive oil in a 12-inch (30.5 cm) skillet over medium heat. Add a finely chopped onion and cook until softened, 4 to 6 minutes. Add in 3 cloves of finely chopped garlic and ½ teaspoon red pepper flakes, season well with salt and black pepper, and cook 1 minute more. Add in 1 can (28 ounces/795 g) whole San Marzano tomatoes and gently crush them with the back of a spoon. Simmer for 20 minutes. Taste and adjust seasonings as needed. Add the gnocchi and gently toss to coat with the sauce. Plate in bowls and shower with more grated pecorino cheese and some roughly chopped fresh herbs such as flat-leaf parsley, basil, or mint.

Chicken and "Dumplings:" Chop and sauté a large leek, carrot, and a few stalks of celery, and thyme if you have it. Season with salt and pepper. Pour in 5 to 6 cups (1.2 to 1.4 L) chicken stock and 2 to 3 cups (390 to 585 g) shredded chicken meat and simmer together for 10 minutes or so. While the soup simmers, bring a large pot of salted water to a boil. Cook the gnocchi. Ladle the soup into bowls and top each with six or so of the "dumplings." Garnish each serving with roughly chopped celery leaves and an optional spoonful of sour cream.

A NOTE: *I did some research on the best way to drain ricotta, but J. Kenji López-Alt, a New York Times food columnist and the Chief Culinary Advisor for Serious Eats, has the simplest and most effective way to do so (as usual). Line a sheet pan or a plate with a few layers of paper towel, spread the cheese onto the paper towel–lined tray and cover with a few more layers of paper towel. Press down to blot any additional moisture. I usually allow the cheese to sit for 20 to 30 minutes. When ready to use, simply remove the top layer of towels and scrape the ricotta into a bowl. Voilà.*

A Sunday Frittata

DURING QUARANTINE, I found myself desperately looking for things I could share with Chad that would become routine, or a cooking ritual that we could repeat on a certain day each week to ground us. I needed something of our own to look forward to and to count on as things were changing so quickly day to day. I pestered him to play board games or rounds of Rummy 500 on weekend afternoons, or even to eat dinner in the dining room each night. But much to my dismay, Chad is not a game player, and most evenings we ended up with food on our laps in front of the television with two bottles of wine to numb another tough day of grief and uncertainty.

One late Sunday morning, without much thought at all, I made a frittata. A reasonable, not at all groundbreaking thing to do on a weekend. Chad sat and sipped coffee at our small table in the kitchen as I rummaged through the fridge to find odds and ends of things that might work well in some eggs. He then toasted and buttered thick slices of sesame sourdough bread while I assembled the frittata, and we then sat together for an early lunch.

The next Sunday I found myself doing it again and then again the weekend after that. One week the frittata incorporated mushrooms, onions, and on-their-way-out herbs. Another was paper-thin sliced potatoes, fried in an ample amount of oil until potato chip crisp, with charred leeks and roasted peppers topped with creamy feta cheese. And on even another, it was finely chopped leftover slices of frozen New Year's Day ham with some cheddar cheese and green onions. I once also accidently added in rice as I didn't realize Chad had stored the leftover roasted vegetables in the same container—no mind, it worked! Really anything can go into a frittata.

Admittedly a little slow on the uptake sometimes, it suddenly struck me that perhaps this was our ritual. It wasn't forced, it just became something that we did because we enjoyed doing it, which, it turns out is an important piece if you're going to keep doing the thing you are doing repeatedly for fun.

I never planned on including a frittata recipe in this book, but then again, I never planned on being stuck at home and social distancing for over a year. So here is one that you can make your own. I hope when you're serving it, you're seated at a table full of friends or family who you're able to wrap your arms around.

A Sunday Frittata

SERVES 6

TIME 20 minutes

INGREDIENTS

8 large eggs

¼ cup (60 ml) heavy cream or half-and-half

Kosher salt and freshly ground black pepper

¼ cup (½ stick/55 g) unsalted butter

1 small yellow onion, thinly sliced

2 cups (60 g) roughly chopped wiltable greens, such as arugula, kale, or spinach (optional)

1 to 1½ cups (128 g to 192 g) additional fillings (see my "Frittata Filling Suggestions" below; optional)

½ cup (55 g) cheese, such as grated cheddar, mozzarella, or provolone or crumbled feta or goat cheese

Handful roughly chopped herbs, such as fresh flat-leaf parsley, dill, or cilantro, for serving (optional)

METHOD

Preheat the oven to 375°F (190°C).

In a medium bowl, gently whisk together the eggs and heavy cream. Season well with salt and pepper and set aside.

In a 10-inch (25 cm) cast-iron or nonstick skillet, melt the butter over medium heat. Add the onion and cook until translucent, 4 to 5 minutes. Season with salt. Add your own additions along with the greens, if using either, and cook until everything is gently cooked and the greens have wilted.

Once you've cooked your fillings, pour in the eggs and turn down the heat to medium-low. Cook for 1 to 2 minutes, until the eggs begin to set. Gently place the pan in the oven and cook until the eggs begin puffing up around the edges, 12 to 14 minutes. Remove from the oven and sprinkle the cheese over the top.

Turn the oven to broil. Place the pan under the broiler and cook until the cheese melts and becomes golden, watching it closely to make sure it doesn't burn, 1 to 2 minutes more.

Remove from the oven and top with roughly chopped herbs, should you like. Cut into wedges and serve warm or at room temperature. Eat all day.

FRITTATA FILLING SUGGESTIONS:

Vegetables: Roasted mushrooms, potatoes, fennel, red peppers, blanched broccoli rabe, cherry tomatoes, or zucchini.

Meat: A lone cooked sausage, diced ham, a strip or two of crisped-up bacon, or leftover braised pork shoulder. I also once finely chopped a thin, leftover cheeseburger patty and threw it in. It was delicious.

Spring Lamb Ragù *with* Anchovies and Pea Shoots

I originally made this dish for an intimate Buona Pasqua dinner. Intimate meaning for myself and Chad. Usually for Easter, we get together with Jenn, Steve, and their daughter Brynn and grill some cut of lamb over open fire, but that particular year was very different due to sheltering in place. Determined not to let it dampen my spirits, I made Chad drive all over town in hunt of forsythia to cut down, to bring some spring into the house and make our dinner feel celebratory—crankily (him) and sadly (me), we came home empty handed. Moments later and completely unprompted, Jenn texted to ask if we'd like some forsythia from her yard and I couldn't believe my luck. Her husband Steve arrived on our porch an hour later, arms full of branches. I quickly put them in water in a big vase on the dining room table and Chad and I sat down to a late-afternoon spring supper of thick egg noodles tossed with lamb, the season's first pea shoots, and lots of butter and herbs. Celebrate we did.

SERVES 4

TIME 35 minutes

INGREDIENTS

2 tablespoons olive oil

1 large leek, trimmed, rinsed of grit, then thinly sliced (about 1½ cups/125 g) or 1 medium yellow onion, finely chopped

Kosher salt

3 cloves garlic, finely chopped

3 oil-packed anchovies

2 teaspoons finely chopped fresh rosemary

1 tablespoon tomato paste

1 pound (455 g) ground lamb

Freshly ground black pepper

½ cup (120 ml) white wine

1½ to 2 cups (360 to 480 ml) chicken stock

12 ounces (340 g) pappardelle or tagliatelle

2 tablespoons unsalted butter

3 ounces (85 g) pea shoots, arugula, or other baby greens

2 teaspoons lemon zest (from 1 large lemon), plus lemon juice for finishing

½ cup (25 g) loosely packed fresh herbs, such as flat-leaf parsley leaves, mint leaves, and snipped chives

Freshly grated pecorino, for serving

(Continued)

METHOD

Heat the olive oil in a deep-sided 12-inch (30.5 cm) skillet or Dutch oven over medium heat. Add the leek and cook until soft and translucent, 4 to 5 minutes. Season with salt.

Stir in the garlic, anchovies, rosemary, and tomato paste and cook until the anchovies have melted and the tomato paste has toasted slightly, 1 to 2 minutes.

Add the lamb and cook, pressing the meat firmly into the bottom of the pan until it begins to crisp up and stirring until it is browned through, 5 to 7 minutes. Season with salt and pepper. Pour in the white wine and cook until it is reduced by half, 3 minutes or so. Pour in 1½ cups (360 ml) of the chicken stock and allow the sauce to simmer, stirring occasionally, while you make the pasta. If it looks like it's drying out, stir in the remaining ½ cup (60 ml) stock.

Bring a large pot of salted water to a boil. Cook the pasta according to package directions, just shy of al dente. Drain the pasta and reserve 1 cup (240 ml) of the cooking water.

Add the pasta to the skillet with the lamb along with the butter and pea shoots. Toss together, adding in a few tablespoons of the reserved pasta cooking water if needed, until the pasta is glossy with sauce, the pea shoots have wilted, and the butter has melted. Add half the herbs, the lemon zest, and a good squeeze of lemon juice and toss again.

Plate in bowls and top with the remaining herbs. Serve with some grated cheese.

Saucy Paccheri *with* Calamari, Sausage, and Breadcrumbs

Paccheri is one of my favorite pasta shapes, likely due to the fact that its generous tube shape makes it perfect for capturing perfectly constructed bites. Loosely translated from Neapolitan, paccheri means "slap," referring to the sound it makes when being eaten, which also makes it endearing. I love pairing seafood and pork together, and so I did in this quick-to-come-together dish. It's finished with breadcrumbs that have been toasted in olive oil for some crunch.

SERVES 4

TIME 30 minutes

INGREDIENTS

4 tablespoons (60 ml) olive oil, plus more for drizzling (optional)

½ cup (25 g) panko breadcrumbs

Flaky salt

10 ounces (280 g) paccheri or rigatoni

Kosher salt

8 ounces (225 g) sweet or spicy Italian sausage, casing removed

1 large shallot, thinly sliced

4 cloves garlic, thinly sliced

Freshly ground black pepper

1 tablespoon tomato paste

1 can (28 ounces/795 g) crushed San Marzano tomatoes

1 pound (455 g) calamari, bodies cut into ¼-inch pieces and tentacles roughly chopped if large

¼ cup (13 g) finely chopped fresh flat-leaf parsley

Flaky salt (optional)

METHOD

In a deep-sided 12-inch (30.5 cm) skillet, heat 2 tablespoons of the olive oil over medium heat until it shimmers then add the breadcrumbs. Toast, stirring occasionally, until the breadcrumbs are golden, 3 to 4 minutes. Set aside in a small bowl and season with flaky salt.

Bring a large pot of water to a boil while you make your sauce. Add a generous amount of kosher salt to the water and, when it comes back to a boil, cook the pasta just shy of the minutes specified in the package directions; you want it a bit more al dente as it will finish cooking in the sauce.

(Continued)

If needed, wipe out the skillet and then heat the remaining 2 tablespoons oil over medium heat. Add the sausage and cook, breaking up the meat with a spatula or the back of a spoon, until crispy, 5 to 7 minutes. Stir in the shallot and garlic and cook 2 minutes more, then season with kosher salt and black pepper.

Stir in the tomato paste and cook for 1 minute or so. Pour in the crushed tomatoes and then add about ½ cup (120 ml) water to the can, swish it around, and add it to the sauce. Bring to a simmer, stirring occasionally so the sauce doesn't stick to the bottom of the pan, while you finish the pasta. If the sauce is getting too thick, stir in a bit of the boiling pasta water.

When the pasta is about 1 to 2 minutes away from being cooked, add the calamari to the sauce and stir to combine. They cook rather quickly, and you don't want them to overcook and turn tough and rubbery.

Drain the pasta, reserving an additional ½ cup (120 ml) of the pasta cooking water. Add the pasta directly to the skillet and toss everything to combine until the pasta is glossy with sauce. Taste and adjust seasoning with kosher salt accordingly. Plate in bowls and top with the reserved breadcrumbs and the parsley. Finish with flaky salt and a drizzle of olive oil if you like.

Broth, Some Fregola, Some Broccoli Rabe, *and* Crispy Prosciutto

In the blustery, cold winter season, I fervently make broth and turn whatever is lurking about in my fridge into soup. This one in particular came about after my friend Kelly and I went out for what we call a "one and done" drink at Rivertown Lodge in town, which actually means three and then I get home and remember I have to make dinner. Endearingly flexible, make this dish your own tipsy (or not) meal by swapping in any wiltable green or grain. Toppings are optional, but never a bad idea.

SERVES 4

TIME 25 minutes

INGREDIENTS

2 tablespoons olive oil

3 ounces (85 g) prosciutto, roughly chopped or torn into 1- to 1½-inch (2.5 to 4 cm) pieces

1 medium yellow onion, finely chopped

1 medium stalk celery, thinly sliced

3 cloves garlic, finely chopped

½ teaspoon red pepper flakes

1 tablespoon tomato paste

Kosher salt

6 cups (1.4 L) chicken stock

½ cup (90 g) fregola or pearled couscous

1 bunch broccoli rabe, roughly chopped into 1-inch (2.5 cm) pieces

Topping suggestions: soft-boiled eggs, Crispy Garlic Chili Oil with Shallots and Fennel Seeds (page 46), roughly chopped celery leaves, freshly grated pecorino or Parmesan cheese

METHOD

In a large Dutch oven or stockpot, heat the olive oil over medium heat. Add the prosciutto and cook, stirring occasionally, until it begins to crisp and brown in spots, 2 to 3 minutes. Remove from the pot and place on a paper towel–lined plate.

Add the onion and the celery to the pot and cook, stirring occasionally until they begin to soften, 4 to 5 minutes. Stir in the garlic, red pepper flakes, and tomato paste and cook for 1 to 2 minutes more. Season well with salt.

Pour in the chicken stock and when it comes to a boil add the fregola and turn down the heat to a simmer. About 5 minutes before the pasta is finished cooking, add the broccoli rabe to the broth and stir until it wilts and cooks down a bit. Taste and adjust seasoning with salt to taste.

Ladle the broth into bowls, making sure you get some fregola and broccoli rabe in each one, and top each portion with some of the crisped-up prosciutto and any of the other toppings I've suggested or that you prefer.

Creamy Risotto *with* Crispy Wild Mushrooms

Yes, you guessed it. This recipe was conceived in my crispy mushroom and desperately seeking anything creamy period. It's very good and worth making even when you're not in the midst of a pandemic. Promise! Serve with lots of wine.

SERVES 4

TIME 40 minutes

INGREDIENTS

8 to 10 cups (2 to 2.4 L) chicken stock, preferably homemade

4 tablespoons (½ stick/55 g) unsalted butter

2 tablespoons olive oil

1¼ pounds (570 g) mixed wild mushrooms, such as cremini, shiitake, maitake, or trumpet, torn or chopped into bite-size pieces

Kosher salt and freshly ground black pepper

2 teaspoons fresh thyme leaves

½ medium yellow onion finely chopped

2 cloves garlic, finely chopped

1½ cups (285 g) Aborio rice

½ cup (120 ml) dry white wine

¼ cup (25 g) freshly grated pecorino cheese, plus more for garnish (optional)

2 tablespoons sour cream, crème fraîche, or mascarpone

¼ cup (13 g) finely chopped fresh flat-leaf parsley, plus more for garnish (optional)

Flaky salt, for finishing

METHOD

In a large Dutch oven or stockpot, bring the chicken stock to a simmer over medium heat.

In another large Dutch oven or deep-sided 12-inch (30.5 cm) skillet, melt 2 tablespoons of the butter and heat the olive oil over medium heat. Add the mushrooms and cook, stirring occasionally, until the mushrooms turn golden and crispy, 12 to 15 minutes. Season well with kosher salt and black pepper and stir in the thyme. Transfer the mushrooms to a medium bowl, setting aside ¼ cup (32 g) for garnish.

If needed, wipe out the pan. Turn down the heat to medium-low and add the remaining 2 tablespoons butter to the pan. When it melts, add the onion and cook, stirring frequently, until they soften, 4 to 5 minutes. Add the garlic and cook for 30 seconds more. Season well with kosher salt.

Add the rice to the pan, stir to coat with the buttery onions, and let the rice toast for 2 to 3 minutes. Stir in the wine and cook until it evaporates, 2 minutes or so.

(Continued)

Begin adding the simmering stock to the rice, about ½ to ¾ cup (120 to 180 ml) at a time, stirring constantly. Repeat with the remaining stock, cooking and stirring until the rice is creamy but still al dente, 30 minutes or so. Taste it along the way so you know where you're at in terms of consistency. You may not need to use all of the stock, but better to have more on hand than less in case you do.

Turn off the heat and stir in the grated cheese and the sour cream until well combined. Stir in the crispy mushrooms and the parsley and season to taste with kosher salt.

Plate in bowls, top each portion with a bit of the reserved crispy mushrooms, and season with flaky salt and more parsley and grated cheese if you like.

My Cec

The original request for this one-pot recipe came from my lovely editor Margaux at the *New York Times*. I've oddly never made pasta e ceci this way before, even though I wrote a whole book on pasta! And, although I'm generally against cooking pasta in the sauce it's served in, I make an exception here. It really works. A lot of readers thought so too as it became one of my most popular dishes in record time! I started affectionately referring to her as "My Cec." I've changed a few ingredients in this version to make it how I would serve it at home, but the best part about this recipe is it relies on pantry ingredients and is incredibly forgiving. Use water in place of stock, use uncased sausage instead of pancetta (or leave the meat out entirely and keep it vegetarian). It's truly a crowd-pleaser of a dish, and on a cold and blustery night it's easy to double, so having friends over and opening a lot of red wine are actually the only two ingredients that aren't optional.

SERVES 4

TIME 30 minutes

INGREDIENTS

2 tablespoons olive oil, plus more for drizzling (optional)

4 ounces (115 g) pancetta, finely diced

1 medium yellow onion, finely chopped

3 cloves garlic, finely chopped

2 teaspoons chopped fresh rosemary

½ teaspoon red pepper flakes

Kosher salt and freshly ground black pepper

1 cup (165 g) diced canned tomatoes with their juices

1 can (15 ounces/430 g) chickpeas, drained and rinsed

3 to 4 cups (720 to 960 ml) chicken stock

1 cup (120 g) ditalini

5 cups (210 g) roughly chopped escarole, dandelion greens, or something else green and wiltable

Freshly grated pecorino cheese, for serving

METHOD

Heat the oil in a large stockpot or Dutch oven over medium heat. Add the pancetta and cook until crispy and golden. Remove with a slotted spoon and set aside on a paper towel–lined plate.

Add the onion and cook, stirring occasionally, until softened but not taking on any color, 4 to 5 minutes. Add the garlic, rosemary, and red pepper flakes and cook 1 minute more. Season well with salt and pepper.

(Continued)

Add the tomatoes and the chickpeas and stir to combine. With a spatula or the back of a spoon, crush about ½ cup (90 g) of the chickpeas so they release some of their creamy texture into the sauce.

Pour in 3 cups of the stock and turn the heat to medium-high; when it comes to a boil, add the ditalini. Cook, stirring frequently to make sure the pasta is not sticking to the bottom of the pan, until the pasta is just short of al dente, about 8 minutes.

Turn down the heat to medium. Add the escarole and the reserved pancetta to the pot and cook until the greens are wilted, 1 to 2 minutes more. The pasta will absorb most of the stock, so feel free to add in ½ to 1 cup (60 to 120 ml) of the remaining chicken stock if you prefer a brothier stew—it's up to you.

Ladle into bowls and top with grated cheese and a drizzle of more olive oil if you please.

A Dirty Bird, page 158.

CHAPTER SEVEN

Chicken Thighs, Some Birds, *and* Two Soups

157-177

A Dirty Bird
(aka Potato Chip Chicken)

This is the brainchild of my husband, Chad. You may know him from his famous garlic bread recipe in *Back Pocket Pasta*. As he knows, I loved cornflake chicken and Shake 'n Bake as a kid, much to my mother's dismay. This version gives a nod to my childhood nostalgia, with some upgrades. Yes, I'm asking you to cover your chicken with potato chips and butter, along with some smoked paprika and brown sugar to really take it there, and I promise you it does. The chicken stays very juicy on the inside and gets crunchy on the outside. I love this chicken. Serve it with a cabbage slaw and some roasted potatoes (yes, more carbs) and, whatever you do, make sure to scrape up the brown bits, extra crisped in the schmaltz, that have formed on the bottom of the sheet pan and steal them for yourself. Otherwise, you'll be fighting over them at the table.

SERVES 4

TIME 1 hour and 25 minutes

INGREDIENTS

1 chicken (3½ to 4 pounds/1.6 to 1.8 kg)

Kosher salt and freshly ground black pepper

5 ounces (140 g) barbeque potato chips, such as the Kettle brand

2 tablespoons unsalted butter, at room temperature

1 teaspoon smoked paprika

2 teaspoons light brown sugar

METHOD

Preheat the oven to 350°F (175°C). Season your bird well with salt and pepper, inside and out, and place it on a nonstick sheet pan or one that is lined with parchment.

In a food processor, pulse the potato chips until they resemble a coarse crumb. Add the butter, smoked paprika, and the sugar to the processor and pulse again to combine. The crumbs should be pretty fine at this point.

Gently press the potato chip crumbs all over the surface of the chicken so it is evenly coated. Roast in the preheated oven until a thermometer registers 165°F (74°C), about 1½ hours. Allow the bird to rest for 10 to 15 minutes. Carve, plate, delight.

Pan-Roasted Chicken Thighs *with* Asparagus and Charred Scallion–Sesame Salsa

Pan-searing chicken thighs before they go in the oven gives them beautiful, golden skin and adds an extra layer of flavor. The asparagus is tossed in the chicken fat and everything goes into the oven together to finish cooking. Feel free to swap in any seasonally appropriate, quick-roasting vegetables for the asparagus, such as snap peas, broccoli, or zucchini. But in my humble opinion, the charred green onion salsa is what makes this dish sing, with its zingy lime, grassy herbs, and barely there brown sugar. I'd eat this sauce on anything. I like spooning it on top and serving it straight from the pan, but you do as you please.

SERVES 4

TIME 35 minutes

INGREDIENTS

FOR THE CHICKEN:

1½ to 2 pounds (680 to 910 g) bone-in, skin-on chicken thighs, at room temperature

Kosher salt and freshly ground black pepper

1 tablespoon canola or grapeseed oil

1 large bunch asparagus, woody ends snapped off and discarded, cut into 2-inch (5 cm) pieces on the bias

FOR THE SALSA:

¼ cup (60 ml) lime juice

½ teaspoon light brown sugar

1 medium jalapeño chile, thinly sliced, seeds removed if you like

8 green onions (about 1 bunch), trimmed and cut in half horizontally

1 cup (40 g) roughly chopped loosely packed fresh cilantro (both leaves and tender stems)

2 teaspoons grated fresh ginger

¼ teaspoon toasted sesame oil

¼ cup (60 ml) olive oil

Kosher salt

Flaky salt and sesame seeds, for serving (optional)

(Continued)

METHOD

Make the chicken: Preheat the oven to 400°F (205°C). Pat the chicken very dry and season well with kosher salt and black pepper.

Heat a 12-inch (30.5 cm) cast-iron pan or other oven-safe skillet over medium-high heat. Add the oil, and when it shimmers, add the chicken, skin side down, and cook undisturbed until it forms a caramelly-golden color, about 5 to 7 minutes. Flip and cook 4 to 5 minutes more. Remove the thighs and set aside on a plate.

Turn off the heat and add the asparagus to the pan, stirring to coat it in the rendered chicken fat, and season with salt and black pepper. Transfer the chicken back to the pan, nestling it in around the asparagus (if some needs to sit right on top that is OK). Roast until the chicken is cooked through and the asparagus is tender, 15 to 20 minutes more.

Meanwhile, prepare the salsa: In a medium bowl, stir together the lime juice, brown sugar, and jalapeño and set aside. Heat a large skillet over medium heat. Add the green onions and cook, tossing frequently, until they begin to blacken and char in spots. Remove and set aside. When cool enough to touch, finely chop the green onions and place them in the bowl with the jalapeños. Stir in the cilantro, ginger, sesame oil, and olive oil and season to taste with kosher salt.

When the chicken is done, remove it from the oven and allow it to rest for 5 minutes or so. Either slice the chicken and return it to the pan or leave it on the bone to deal with at the table. Spoon most of the salsa directly over the chicken and asparagus and season with flaky salt and sesame seeds. Pass the remaining salsa at the table.

Indian-Spiced Yogurt Chicken *with* Quick Pickled Onion and Herbs

When I lived in Brooklyn, we ordered Indian food once a week. In fact, I love it so much that one year I threw myself a thirty-person Indian-inspired potluck birthday party—it was a lot of fun. Now that I live in Hudson, the only authentic Indian food is about a thirty-minute drive away. So these days when I'm craving flavors such as these, I try to take matters into my own hands. This sheet pan variation is a nod to tandoori chicken. I use boneless chicken thighs in this version as they cook quickly, but if you'd prefer bone-in thighs by all means feel free to use them, just increase the cooking time by 15 to 20 minutes. The quick pickled onions are similar to a condiment that is usually found in my takeout satchel, plus they give the dish an acidic punch—and they look pretty too.

SERVES 4

TIME 45 minutes

INGREDIENTS

½ medium red onion, thinly sliced

2 tablespoons good-quality white wine vinegar

Pinch kosher salt

1 cup (240 ml) full-fat yogurt

1 large clove garlic, grated

2 teaspoons grated fresh ginger

2 teaspoons light brown sugar

1 teaspoon ground cumin

1 teaspoon ground coriander

1 teaspoon turmeric

1 tablespoon garam masala

Kosher salt and freshly ground black pepper

2 pounds (910 g) boneless chicken thighs

½ cup (20 g) finely chopped mixed fresh herbs, such as cilantro, mint, or green onions

METHOD

In a small bowl, toss the onions with the vinegar and a good pinch of salt and set aside.

In a large bowl, stir together the yogurt, garlic, ginger, and brown sugar, with the cumin, coriander, turmeric, and garam masala. Season well with salt and black pepper. Add the chicken thighs and toss to coat evenly in the marinade. Let sit at room temperature for about 30 minutes or overnight in the fridge.

Preheat the oven to 425°F (220°C). Scrape off any additional marinade from the chicken thighs and place them in a single layer on a large rimmed sheet pan. Bake until the chicken is almost cooked through, 15 to 18 minutes. Turn the heat to broil and cook for 1 to 2 minutes more, until the chicken is brown and golden in places. Toss the herbs with the chicken on the pan. Transfer to a platter, scatter with the pickled onions, and serve.

Chicken Quintiliano

The original recipe for this dish has been in our family for more than eighty years. The name comes from my late nonni's friend Luigi Quintiliano, who passed it down to her. I use two kinds of vinegar, but the dish would work with one or the other, just make sure it's good quality. Using boneless, skinless chicken thighs allows the dish to come together quickly; if you want to swap in bone-in thighs please do, but add an additional 15 to 20 minutes cooking time. I've kept this recipe simple to honor its tradition, but one could also crisp some pancetta before the garlic goes in, or alternatively add in a few anchovies to melt. This dish is flexible and flavorful and perfect for a quick, cozy dinner at home.

SERVES 4

TIME 25 minutes

INGREDIENTS

2 pounds (190 g) boneless, skinless chicken thighs

Kosher salt and freshly ground black pepper

3 tablespoons olive oil

8 to 10 cloves garlic, peeled and smashed with the back of a knife

½ cup (120 ml) good quality balsamic vinegar

½ cup (120 ml) good quality red wine vinegar

2 sprigs oregano or marjoram

½ cup (25 g) finely chopped fresh flat-leaf parsley

Flaky salt, for serving

Polenta, rice, or mashed potatoes, for serving

METHOD

Season the chicken well with kosher salt and black pepper. In a large sauté pan, heat the olive oil over medium heat. Add the garlic cloves and cook until they they start to become fragrant and golden, about 2 to 3 minutes. Remove and set aside.

Begin cooking the chicken thighs in batches, making sure not to crowd the pan. Cook until the chicken is no longer pink on the outside and begins to lightly brown in spots, 3 to 4 minutes per side. If it's not cooked through at this point, it's ok.

Return all the chicken thighs and their juices to the pan. Pour in the balsamic and red wine vinegars and bring to a simmer. Add the oregano and the reserved garlic and cover the pan. Allow the meat to finish cooking in the sauce, about 7 minutes more.

Uncover and toss the chicken to coat with the sauce. Cook the chicken for 2 to 3 minutes more, until the sauce has reduced by about half. Sprinkle with parsley, season with flaky salt, and serve with polenta, rice, or mashed potatoes.

A NOTE: *I Googled Luigi and stumbled across his obituary in the New York Times. Like my nonni, he was an organizer for the International Ladies Garment Workers Union. Even more fascinating was that he was a defense witness in the Sacco and Vanzetti trial and an anti-fascist activist. He was married to Angela Bambace, the first Italian-American immigrant woman to hold a leadership position in the ILGWU. Unlike Luigi, she has a Wikipedia page.*

Spatchcocked Lime Pickle Roasted Chicken

This idea for this recipe came about over a dinner party with our friends Eva and Bobby. Partial to the addictively salty and spicy lime pickle frequently at the table alongside Indian dishes, we were brainstorming other ways to use our favorite condiment. We landed on a roasted chicken and, after many variations, I'm certain you'll be pleased. This bird stands out from the rest, and it is roasted on lower heat than normal to ensure fall-off-the-bone meat packed with flavor. If you can salt and pepper your chicken and refrigerate it overnight, it will result in an even juicer bird. Leftovers make for a very good chicken salad sandwich tossed with green onions and cilantro leaves and tender stems.

SERVES 4

TIME 1 hour and 15 minutes

INGREDIENTS

1 chicken (3½ to 4 pounds/1.6 to 1.8 kg)

Kosher salt and freshly ground black pepper

3 small shallots (about 2½ ounces/70 g), halved and peeled

3 cloves garlic, peeled

2 tablespoons olive oil

1 teaspoon curry powder

⅓ cup (80 g) lime pickle (available at Indian groceries or online)

METHOD

With a pair of kitchen shears, cut along one side of the chicken's backbone. Repeat on the other side of the bird and remove the bone entirely (see note). Press down firmly on the breast of the bird to crack the wishbone so the chicken lies flat. Set on a rimmed sheet pan lined with parchment paper or a well-seasoned cast-iron pan and season with salt and pepper.

Preheat the oven to 350°F (175°C). In a bowl, toss the shallots and garlic cloves with 1 tablespoon of the olive oil. Roast in a small pan until they just begin to soften, 12 to 15 minutes.

Put the roasted shallots and garlic in a food processor. Add curry powder and lime pickle and pulse until a paste forms. Spread the mixture evenly all over the skin side of the chicken. Drizzle with the remaining tablespoon of olive oil.

Roast the chicken at 350°F (175°C) until an instant-read thermometer inserted into the thickest part of the thigh registers 165°F (74°C), about 1 hour. Remove from the oven and let the chicken rest for about 10 minutes before carving.

A NOTE: *Save the backbone of that bird; it makes for flavorful stocks. I keep a big ziptight bag of miscellaneous bones in my freezer so I can make broth whenever the mood strikes. When I've done nothing else with my day except let bones and vegetables simmer in a large pot, it makes me feel very accomplished. You will too.*

Skillet Chicken *with* Wilted Radicchio, Anchovy, and Onion

I'm not going to lie: If I can make something in one pan, I certainly will. Not only am I the cook in our household, I'm also usually the dishwasher, so if I can cut down on post-dinner sink time, I'm all for it. For that reason, a cast-iron pan is one of my best friends in the kitchen, and it should also be one of yours. When taken care of and seasoned well, it acts as a nonstick skillet and offers a plancha or griddle-like quality; it also distributes heat like a dream for even cooking. Once the thighs are nice and golden, the rest of this dish comes together in no time. I like using Treviso radicchio when it's available, but anything that wilts works.

SERVES 4 to 6

TIME 30 minutes

INGREDIENTS

6 to 8 bone-in, skin-on chicken thighs, about 2½ pounds (1.2 kg)

Kosher salt and freshly ground black pepper

2 tablespoons canola or grapeseed oil

1 medium yellow onion, thinly sliced

3 cloves garlic, thinly sliced

4 to 6 anchovies

3 to 4 Calabrian chiles or ½ teaspoon or more red pepper flakes

2 large bunches Treviso radicchio or other chicory (about 1¼ pounds/20 ounces), roughly chopped

Good-quality balsamic or white wine vinegar, for drizzling, or a squeeze of lemon

Good-quality olive oil, for drizzling (optional)

¼ cup (13 g) roughly chopped fresh flat-leaf parsley or basil or both

METHOD

Season the chicken well with salt and pepper. Heat a 12-inch (30.5 cm) cast-iron pan over medium-high heat for 2 to 3 minutes until very hot. Add the oil, and when it shimmers, add the chicken skin side down (working in batches if needed) and cook undisturbed for 7 to 8 minutes, until the skin becomes a deep golden brown. Flip and cook the chicken 6 to 7 minutes more, or until cooked through. Set aside on a plate.

Pour off all but 2 tablespoons of the chicken fat and oil and return the pan to the stovetop over medium-low heat. Add the onion and cook until it begins to soften, 3 to 4 minutes. Season with salt and pepper. Stir in the garlic, anchovies, and chiles and cook until the garlic turns golden and the anchovies melt, 1 to 2 minutes more.

Add the radicchio to the pan and gently toss it until it's as wilted as you please. Taste and adjust the seasoning with salt accordingly. Drizzle the radicchio with the vinegar and olive oil (if using), add the chicken back to the pan, and top with the herbs. Serve in the pan or on a plate.

Roasted Tomatillo and Poblano Soup *with* Shredded Chicken

My friend Kevin introduced me to a version of this Mexican soup when he briefly lived with my roommate Suzy and I, on our couch in Brooklyn in 2006. That's how we first met and we've been very close ever since. Kevin brought a Sunday dinner tradition and this signature dish to our group of friends, which I will treasure forever and still re-create at home. Over the years, I abandoned the original recipe, which is tucked somewhere, and started making it from memory, adding a few new ingredients here and there as it evolved. I also have fun with the toppings and set out bowls filled with lots of options and let guests have at it.

SERVES 4

TIME 50 minutes

INGREDIENTS

1½ pounds (680 g) tomatillos, husked, rinsed, and halved or quartered if large

3 medium poblano chiles, halved lengthwise, stems and seeds discarded

2 jalapeño chiles, halved lengthwise, stems and seeds discarded

4 tablespoons (60 ml) olive oil

Kosher salt

1 medium yellow onion, chopped

2 cloves garlic, chopped

6 cups (1.4 L) chicken stock

3½ cups (685 g) shredded leftover or store bought rotisserie chicken

An assortment of toppings: roughly chopped fresh cilantro, Fritos or tortilla chips, thinly sliced radishes, green onions, and cotija cheese or sour cream

METHOD

Preheat the oven to 400°F (205°C). On a large rimmed sheet pan, toss together the tomatillos, poblanos, and jalapeños with 2 tablespoons of the oil and season well with salt. Roast, flipping halfway through, until the tomatillos have collapsed and the peppers have softened and begun to lightly brown in spots, 20 to 25 minutes. When cool enough to touch, peel the poblanos, and then roughly chop them along with the jalapeños.

Heat the remaining 2 tablespoons of oil in a large stockpot over medium heat. Add the onion and garlic and cook until the onion has softened and the garlic is fragrant, 2 to 3 minutes. Add the tomatillos and any juices that have been released along with the peppers and stir to coat. Season with salt. Pour in the chicken stock and bring to a simmer. Cook, allowing the flavors to get to know each other, for 10 to 15 minutes.

Using an immersion blender (or working in batches in a standing blender), pulse together until smooth. Stir in the chicken to warm through and adjust seasoning with salt.

Ladle into bowls and garnish with toppings.

It's Almost Spring Stew *with* Chicken and Farro

Like many soups and stews, this recipe is forgiving and can change with the seasons. I first made it when I was craving spring vegetables and there was still a chill in the air. It's a perfect vehicle to use whatever vegetables are lurking about in your fridge. Here, nutty farro is slightly toasted and simmered in chicken broth along with chicken thighs and spring vegetables, which are added in at the end until just snappy, making for a quick-to-come-together supper. Feel free to swap an onion for a leek; chard, arugula, or kale for spinach; and use whatever other vegetables you have around that need using up. It will all be more than fine, I promise. Serve in deep bowls with bread and wine.

SERVES 4 to 6

TIME 45 minutes

INGREDIENTS

½ Meyer lemon, seeded and finely chopped, peel and all

3 tablespoons roughly chopped or torn fresh mint

2 tablespoons olive oil, plus more for drizzling

1 large leek, white and tender green parts, thinly sliced

1 medium fennel bulb, tough outer leaves and stems discarded, thinly sliced crosswise

2 stalks celery, thinly sliced

2 cloves garlic, thinly sliced

Kosher salt and freshly ground black pepper

1 cup (200 g) farro, rinsed

6 cups (240 ml) chicken broth, preferably homemade

12 ounces (240 g) boneless, skinless chicken thighs

5 cups (100 g) loosely packed baby spinach or other tender greens

8 ounces (225 g) snap peas, strings removed

Flaky salt, for serving (optional)

METHOD

In a small bowl, stir together the lemon and mint and set aside.

In a large stockpot or Dutch oven, heat the olive oil over medium heat. Add the leeks, fennel, and celery and cook, stirring frequently, until the vegetables are softened but not browned, 4 to 5 minutes. Add the garlic and cook until fragrant, 1 to 2 minutes more. Season with salt and black pepper.

(Continued)

Stir in the farro and cook until it begins to toast and smell nutty, 2 to 3 minutes. Pour in the stock, add the chicken, and bring to a boil. Reduce the heat to a simmer and cook until the chicken has cooked through and is no longer pink, 10 to 12 minutes, skimming off any bits of foam that float to the surface. Using tongs, transfer the chicken to a cutting board. When cool enough to touch, shred the chicken into bite-size pieces and set aside.

Continue simmering the soup until the farro is toothsome, about 20 minutes more. Add the chicken, spinach, and the snap peas to the pot and cook until the spinach is just wilted and the peas still have some snap, 1 to 2 minutes. Taste and adjust the seasoning with salt as needed.

Ladle into bowls and top with the Meyer lemon and mint mixture. Drizzle with more olive oil and season with flaky salt if you like.

Crispy Chicken Thighs *with* Schmaltzy Potatoes, Red Pepper, and Onion

Oddly there are no boneless, skin-on chicken thighs available for purchase at the grocery store, which makes no sense to me. Clearly the skin is the best part. You can certainly ask a butcher to debone the thighs for you, but chef and friend Kelly Mariani taught me the invaluable tip of taking matters into my own hands. Flip the chicken so it is skin-side down. With a very sharp paring knife, trim any excess fat. Insert the knife on the left side of the bone to create an incision and gently scrape the bone away from the flesh. Repeat on the right side until there is space under the bone. Slip the knife underneath the bone, scraping and working your way up to the top to detach it, removing any cartilage, and repeat at the bottom of the bone. You'll thank me for very crispy skin!

SERVES 4

TIME 45 minutes

INGREDIENTS

2½ pounds (1.2 g) skin-on chicken thighs (about 6), de-boned (see Note)

Kosher salt and freshly ground black pepper

1 tablespoon canola or grapeseed oil

1 medium onion, thinly sliced

1 pound (455 g) Yukon gold potatoes, sliced into ¼-inch-thick rounds

2 bell peppers (red, orange, or yellow), thinly sliced

3 cloves garlic, finely chopped

¼ cup (10 g) mixed torn fresh herbs, such as basil, parsley, or mint, for garnish

Crispy Garlic Chili Oil with Shallots and Fennel Seeds (page 46), for drizzling (optional)

METHOD

Preheat the oven to 425°F (220°C).

Season the chicken well with salt and pepper. In a cold 12-inch (30.5 cm) cast-iron skillet, add the oil and then the chicken thighs, skin side down. Turn the stovetop to medium-high heat and cook until the fat renders out of the thighs and the skin is crispy, 12 to 14 minutes. Do not flip the chicken. Remove from the pan and set aside.

Turn the heat down to medium and add the onion, potatoes, and peppers to the skillet, tossing well to coat in the chicken fat. Cook until the onion has softened, 4 to 6 minutes. Stir in the garlic and cook 1 minute more. Season the vegetables with salt and pepper.

(Continued)

Place the chicken thighs on top of the potato mixture, skin side up, and finish cooking in the oven, about 20 minutes more, or until a meat thermometer registers 165°F (74°C) .

If the chicken is finished cooking but you'd like your potatoes crispier, set the chicken asideand broil 2 to 3 minutes, watching carefully to make sure the potatoes do not burn.

Serve together with a showering of herbs on top and a drizzle of Crispy Garlic Chili Oil with Shallots and Fennel Seeds (page 46) if you like.

CHAPTER EIGHT

When Cooking *on* Vacation

179-197

When Cooking on Vacation

I'm not one to book a resort vacation or really even a hotel room, although I'm sure that must be lovely . . . Chad is always asking when we'll book that sort of vacation and someone will finally bring him a drink. He hasn't quite realized it's not likely to happen—but, I'll have a rosé, please. And dear, make it a good pour.

No, friends, I want quite the opposite vacation. Give me a basic kitchen and a charcoal Weber grill and I am hot to trot. No matter the kitchen, I just want to cook in it, visit the markets that surround it, and feel for a brief week (or two if I'm very lucky) that no matter where I lay my head, I am home.

Depending on the destination, I may very well pack my 12-inch (30.5 cm) cast-iron pan, olive oil, flaky salt, and a pair or two of tongs. If I'm not going too far, the remnants of my fridge will likely make their way into a cooler. There are always gems to be found in those crisper drawers. I realize this may not be very practical if I'm going to the south of France. But generally I end up in a kitchen that is adequately assembled. And if I don't, I'm happy shelling out thirty dollars on a hibachi grill I'll leave behind for the next lucky guest or cooking over a fire pit, which makes everything feel more special anyway. You don't need much to pull together beautiful, simple meals.

The thing I love most about vacation cooking is that it's easy. You make do with what you have and use up what's left over, which I find to be a fun game. On my trips, there are days of eating leftover cold fried chicken with gin and tonics on the deck for late-afternoon lunches, as well as sipping on dark, bitter beer and eating Triscuits topped with sharp cheddar cheese. Equally acceptable is snacking on Cape Cod potato chips and drinking Manzanilla sherry while you talk about what to assemble for your next meal. This can go on for a number of hours if you let it, so be mindful. If mosquitos suddenly start nipping at your ankles, it means it's now dusk and you've eaten at least two bags of chips. It happens. But how about that tan?! Can you hear my blissful sigh? Yes, of course you can, but let's talk about dinner.

In my life, these suppers often happen in summer and hopefully by some salt water, which makes your access to fish easy—that is if you like fish, which I hope you do. Olive oil, salt, pepper, some high heat, and fresh herbs for a salsa verde and you've created a masterpiece.

Leftovers can be turned into a fish dip, or, with some rice, a sort of kedgeree, or perhaps a Niçoise-ish salad with the addition of leftover bean or potato salad, thick wedges of tomatoes plentifully doused in oil, and a few hard-boiled eggs. All very nice ideas and you've barely lifted a finger.

If you've deemed a "let them eat steak" night, you are also set up for success for the next day. Thinly sliced steak on toasted bread spread generously with butter, which is given an equally freehanded swipe of aioli and then topped with peppery watercress, is a fine, elegant sandwich. If there are cooking juices left over from the night before that can be gently warmed, it would not be a terrible idea to spoon them on top to gently wilt the bitter greens. When paired with a cold beer, this makes for a lovely light evening meal.

Of course, I hope there are some nights you'll want to project cook. These are also fun. The whole day is devoted to planning, shopping, and prepping, which I find to be very enjoyable. It gives vacation without a beach a purpose. Once, while staying at a farmhouse in Provence, we had a potluck with our neighbors (the owners of the house) for twelve people. I made beef stew, they made individual potato gratins and collaboratively drank them out of their rosé. On another night, I roasted a leg of lamb and potatoes in its fat. Both made for great leftovers to eat while hungover the next day (oh, France). *Ça va bien*.

All of this is to say: By committing to cook on vacation, you're creating a temporary place to call your very own, which I find to be the ultimate luxury.

Creamy Clams *with* Leeks and Herbs

This is most certainly a quite languorous version of clam chowder, best served by the sea in whatever season you like to be by it. Cozied up in a worn-in Irish fisherman sweater around a fire with bowls of creamy clams in hand sounds rather nice. Feel free to fry a few pieces of diced bacon in lieu of the butter, or swap in mussels for the clams or use a combination of both. Your choice of herbs, too, is very much up to you. Tarragon and chervil would work well. Drink wine alongside and plenty of it, and your laziness will suddenly feel like anything but.

SERVES 4

TIME 15 minutes

INGREDIENTS

¼ cup (½ stick/55 g) unsalted butter

1 large leek, white and pale green parts only, thinly sliced (about 1½ cups/133.5 g)

2 ribs celery, thinly sliced, plus ¼ cup (7.5 g) celery leaves, roughly chopped, for garnish

1 tablespoon fresh thyme leaves

Kosher salt

¾ cup (180 ml) dry white wine

4 pounds (1.8 kg) manilla or littleneck clams, scrubbed

1 cup (240 ml) heavy cream

Freshly ground black pepper

¼ cup (11 g) finely chopped chives

Lemon wedges, for serving (optional)

4 slices thick country bread, grilled or toasted, for serving

METHOD

In a large Dutch oven or high-sided skillet, melt the butter over medium heat. Add the leek and celery and cook until soft and translucent (don't allow them to take on any color), 3 to 4 minutes. Stir in the thyme and season sparingly with salt—the clams are plenty salty on their own.

Pour in the wine and bring to a simmer. Add the clams, cover, and cook, shaking the pan occasionally, until the clams pop open, 6 to 8 minutes. Discard any clams that have not opened.

Turn off the heat and pour in the cream, stirring until it is warmed through. Season liberally with pepper and garnish with the celery leaves and the chives. Squeeze lemon juice over the top if you like and serve in bowls alongside grilled or toasted bread.

More Shrimp Than You *Think* Pasta

On one summer trip to Montauk, we were lucky that our friend Susan also happened to be in town. She's been spending summers out there for thirty years and knows everything you need to know. Each day was similar. After an extended afternoon at the beach filled with turkey and Swiss cheese sandwiches, potato chips, and watery, ice cold beer, we'd make our way to the Montauket (my favorite bar on earth) for sundowners before puttering home so I could assemble dinner. One particular evening I was craving pasta, a surprise to no one, but I wanted a dish that let the shrimp be the star as opposed to it being overwhelmed by noodles, so I cut the "traditional" pasta portion in half. I think a pound is generally too much to serve four anyway. I also decided that in order to construct the bite I envisioned, I'd need to chop the shrimp so it could be captured perfectly within the tube of pasta. Luckily it was a success.

SERVES 4

TIME 30 minutes

INGREDIENTS

Kosher salt

8 ounces (225 g) mezzi rigatoni or other tubular shaped pasta

½ cup (1 stick/115 g) unsalted butter

1 teaspoon fennel seeds

1 medium fennel bulb, tough outer leaves and stems trimmed and discarded, thinly sliced crosswise

1 medium red or yellow onion, halved and thinly sliced

3 cloves garlic, thinly sliced

2 chile peppers, such as cayenne, serrano, or Fresno, thinly sliced, seeds removed if you like

1½ pounds (680 g) large wild shrimp, peeled, deveined, and tails removed, cut into ½-inch (12 mm) pieces

Freshly ground black pepper

1 cup (240 ml) dry white wine

8 ounces (225 g) baby arugula, spinach, or other tender greens

1 cup (40 g) roughly chopped tender herbs, such as basil and mint

Lemon, for serving

Flaky salt, for finishing (optional)

METHOD

Bring a large pot of well-salted water to a boil. Add the pasta and cook according to package directions, until it is just short of al dente. Drain, reserving 1 cup (240 ml) of the pasta cooking water.

While the pasta cooks, make your sauce. Melt 4 tablespoons (½ stick/55 g) of the butter in a deep-sided 12-inch (30.5 cm) skillet over medium heat. Add the fennel seeds and cook until they become fragrant and golden, 1 to 2 minutes.

(Continued)

Add the fresh fennel, red onion, garlic, and chiles to the pan and season with kosher salt. Cook, stirring occasionally, until the vegetables are softened, 2 to 3 minutes. Pour in the wine and simmer until the liquid is reduced by half, 3 to 5 minutes. Stir in the shrimp, season with kosher salt and black pepper, and cook until they are just cooked through, 1 to 2 minutes.

Add the pasta to the skillet and toss to coat with the sauce. Add the arugula, ½ cup (120 ml) of the reserved pasta water, and the remaining 4 tablespoons (½ stick/55 g) butter and toss well, until the butter is melted, the arugula is wilted, and the pasta is glossy with sauce. Stir in a tablespoon more or so of the pasta water if you want your pasta a little saucier. Top with the herbs and a good squeeze of lemon juice. Serve in bowls and season with flaky salt if desired.

"Gin and Tonicas" *with* Salty Snacks

Chad and I drink "gin and tonicas" in the summer and by the gobletful. That's how we had them in Madrid (and what they, and we now, call them) and we've been making them this way ever since. We love using Máhon gin, which is made in Menorca and is the only gin with a DOC. It's particularly piney in flavor, so it's best mixed with tonic and not used in negronis. No collins glass or limes in our version either. We take ours with crushed ice in a deep wineglass with a big wedge of lemon. On a porch, on a deck, or on a dock, there is no denying this is a sublime sundowner. I enjoy this with potato chips, triscuits and cheddar cheese, pretzels, cold fried chicken, or something else you deem appropriately salty and snacky.

SERVES 2

TIME 5 minutes

INGREDIENTS

Crushed iced

6 ounces (180 ml) gin, such as Máhon or Hendricks (more botanical), Beefeater (straight-up dry), or Plymouth (earthier)

8 ounces (240 ml) tonic water

2 lemon wedges, for serving

METHOD

Fill two large goblet-like wineglasses with crushed ice.

Add 3 ounces (90 ml) gin to each glass (I like them stiff, what can I say?) and top with the tonic. Stir and squeeze a lemon wedge into each glass, then stir again and serve.

Summer Fish *with* Garlic Scapes and Flowering Herbs

I call this summer fish because I made it one late June when we were visiting the south shore of Nova Scotia for the very first time. I've never fallen for a place so hard, so fast! It's magical. The house we were staying in didn't have much kitchen equipment, but luckily I had packed my well-seasoned cast-iron pan, which works well for preparing this dish. Earlier that day in town, we had visited a fish store named Dory Mates Seafood Shop, which had just been opened by a woman named Kelly. She recommended the local halibut and I couldn't refuse. We found herbs and garlic scapes at the Lunenburg farmers market and a vacation dinner easily pieced itself together. If halibut is not available, cod or haddock would also work.

SERVES 4

TIME 25 minutes

INGREDIENTS

3 ounces (85 g) garlic scapes

¼ cup (10 g) loosely packed, roughly chopped or torn fresh basil leaves

3 tablespoons roughly chopped flowering herbs, such as chives or thyme

¾ cup (180 ml) olive oil

Kosher salt

1 lemon, for the herb oil and for serving

4 halibut fillets (6 ounces/170 g each) or 2 bone-in halibut steaks (14 to 16 ounces/400 to 455 g each), 1 to 1¼ inches thick (2.5 to 3 cm)

Freshly ground black pepper

2 tablespoons grapeseed or canola oil

Flaky salt, for serving (optional)

METHOD

Heat a 12-inch (30.5 cm) skillet, preferably cast-iron, over medium-high heat until very hot, 2 to 3 minutes. Add the garlic scapes and cook until they begin to turn golden and char in spots, 3 to 5 minutes. Remove to a cutting board and when cool enough to touch, roughly chop into ½-inch (12 mm) pieces.

In a medium bowl, gently stir together the garlic scapes, basil, and flowering herbs with the olive oil. Season with salt to taste and a squeeze of lemon and set aside.

Season the halibut well with kosher salt and black pepper. Wipe out the skillet if necessary and heat the pan over medium-high heat until very hot, 2 to 3 minutes. Add the grapeseed oil and, when it shimmers, add the halibut fillets and cook undisturbed until they begin to turn golden brown, about 3 to 4 minutes. Flip and finish cooking, about 3 minutes more. Allow 2 to 3 minutes more per side if using halibut steaks.

Serve the fish in the pan or on a platter and spoon the herb oil over the top. Squeeze lemon juice over the top and season with flaky salt if you please.

Clams Avellino

My friend and fellow cookbook author Carla Lalli Music and her family rented the same house in Montauk for many years and, many a late July, Chad and I would drive to join them for a summer dinner. Carla and I met working in the magazine world and have been close for more than a decade now. Our real bond came about when we realized that our families hail from the same part of Italy, a small province about an hour outside of Naples called Avellino, where basil and tomatoes grow with abandon. We made a version of these clams together one summer night and drank Campari and sodas barefoot on the deck. I encourage you to do the same.

SERVES 4

TIME 20 minutes

INGREDIENTS

2 tablespoons olive oil

3 cloves garlic, thinly sliced

1 fresh chile pepper, such as cayenne or serrano, thinly sliced, or ½ teaspoon red pepper flakes

1¼ pounds (570 g) heirloom cherry tomatoes, halved if large

¾ cup (180 ml) dry white wine

4 pounds (1.8 kg) littleneck clams, scrubbed and rinsed

1 cup (40 g) loosely packed fresh basil leaves (torn if large)

Toasted or grilled bread, for serving (optional)

METHOD

In a large pot with a lid or a Dutch oven, heat the oil over medium heat. Add the garlic and the chile pepper and cook, stirring frequently, until the garlic is just golden and everything is fragrant, 1 to 2 minutes. Add the tomatoes and cook until they start to burst and become jammy, 5 to 7 minutes, pressing down on them with a spatula or spoon gently to help them along if needed.

Stir in the white wine, add the clams, and raise the heat to bring to a simmer. Cover and cook, shaking the pan occasionally, until the clams pop open, 6 to 8 minutes. Discard any clams that have not opened.

Scatter the clams with basil leaves and serve straight from the pot on the table or spoon into bowls with plenty of toasted or grilled bread on the side for sopping.

A NOTE: *I know what you're thinking. Colu, there are two steamed clam recipes in this chapter—and you would be correct, there are. I love clams! Clam pasta, clam toast, grilled clams! Side note, but I once burned my hand pretty badly grilling clams over open fire, but I'd do it again because I love clams that much. Clams, xo.*

Lobster Salad *on* a Bun or Not

It isn't summer without eating lobster at least once, or a number of times if you are so fortunate. And so, on the beloved ramshackle deck that looks onto the Peconic, attached to the house my dad rents in Hampton Bays, this salad came to be. It's a simple lobster salad, but I like to treat myself and take the extra step of making aioli for it. I've given instructions on how to cook your lobster below, but to save on time, you can have your fishmonger do it for you. I like eating this salad on soft, tender lettuces with an assortment of items surrounding it, such as thick wedges of tomato, avocado, jammy eggs, and blanched green beans, with some more aioli on the side for dipping. Chad likes his served on a toasted buttered bun. However you like to eat it, please do so outside, overlooking the water.

SERVES 4

TIME 45 minutes

INGREDIENTS

Kosher salt

1 pound (455 g) lobster meat, picked from four 1½-pound (680 g) lobsters or eight 3-ounce (85 g) tails

3 to 4 tablespoons (45 to 60 ml) Aioli (page 47) or mayonnaise

1 medium stalk celery, thinly sliced

2 tablespoons roughly chopped fresh tarragon

2 teaspoons minced fresh chives

1 lemon halved

Your choice of soft butter lettuce, wedges of tomato, avocado, jammy eggs, blanched string beans, or toasted buttered buns, for serving

METHOD

Bring a large pot of heavily salted water to a boil. Drop the lobster in the pot (if you are boiling whole lobsters, you will need to do these two at a time) and cook until the shells are bright red and the meat is opaque, 9 to 10 minutes. If you're using tails, they take 5 to 6 minutes to cook. Remove and place on a rimmed sheet pan to cool.

With kitchen shears, a mallet, or lobster crackers, crack the shells and remove the meat, slicing it into ½- to ¾-inch (12 mm to 2 cm) pieces. I like to keep them on the larger end. Luxury!

In a bowl, gently toss together the lobster meat with the aioli until just combined. I don't like the dressing to be overly clingy, as it can overpower the sweetness of the lobster meat, which is the star.

Add the celery, tarragon, and chives and toss again. Season to taste with salt and the lemon juice.

Serve on a platter with soft butter lettuce and wedges of tomato, avocado, jammy eggs, and blanched string beans, or be like Chad and put it on a toasted buttered bun.

Adrian's Cheladas

On a girls' trip to Zihuatanejo, Mexico, I ordered a michelada and instead was given this brilliant version, which is in the same family, but I'd never had the pleasure of drinking it before. A sweetheart of a gentleman named Adrian made them for us and I lost my mind! It was incredibly refreshing, bright, and almost felt good for me in an electrolyte-type of way. I'll tell myself anything to justify one more beer . . . . It is the most perfect drink for a hot day, and so I asked Adrian if he'd show me how he made them and, luckily for all of us, he did. This is my take. Serve with chips and guacamole and a plunge pool on the side.

SERVES 4

TIME 10 minutes

INGREDIENTS

1 teaspoon kosher salt, plus more for the rims of the glasses

1 cup (240 ml) freshly squeezed lime juice (from 8 limes), plus ½ lime for the salt rim

4 (12-ounce/360 ml) Mexican lagers, such as Dos Equis, Tecate, or Modelo

Ice cubes, as needed

METHOD

Pour some salt onto a small plate. Rub a cut lime around the rims of four pint glasses and then dip each glass into the salt to coat the rim.

Pour ¼ cup (60 ml) of the lime juice into each glass, then slowly pour one beer into each glass. Gently stir an additional ¼ teaspoon salt into each glass.

Add ice, stir again, and serve.

Steak Sandwiches on Buttered Toast *with* Aioli and Spicy Greens

Of course you can make this sandwich with leftover steak. But it's also worthy of a deliberate meal on a hot summer night when you've been at the beach all day. As with any simple dish, quality ingredients are key, so make sure you buy a good steak and your favorite bread. If you read the "For Embellishment" chapter of this book, your aioli should already be in the fridge. If it's not, I highly recommend making it for this sandwich. But, if it is ten P.M. by the time you've gotten around to making dinner, I will forgive you if you make do. Simply place some Hellmann's in a bowl and stir in a grated garlic clove and a good squeeze of lemon. You're off the hook.

SERVES 2

TIME 20 minutes

INGREDIENTS

1 12 ounce (340 g) boneless New York strip steak, at room temperature

Kosher salt and freshly ground black pepper

Unsalted butter at room temperature

1 tablespoon olive oil

4 (½-inch/12 mm) slices country-style bread or pain de mie

4 tablespoons Aioli (page 47) or mayonnaise

Flaky salt, for finishing

½ cup (20 g) watercress or baby arugula

METHOD

Season the steak well with salt and black pepper. Heat a large cast-iron pan over medium-high heat until very hot, 2 to 3 minutes. Add the oil and when it shimmers, add the steak and let it cook, undisturbed, until it begins to crisp and brown, 3 to 4 minutes. Flip and finish cooking, 2 to 3 minutes more, or until a meat thermometer inserted in the thickest part reads 130°F (55°C) for medium-rare. Set aside and allow the steak to rest for 10 minutes, then slice it very thinly.

Turn the oven to broil and generously butter each slice of bread. Place in the oven buttered side up and toast until golden, 2 to 3 minutes.

Place the toast on a work surface, buttered sides down, and generously swipe the other sides with the aioli.

Evenly divide the steak between 2 slices of the toasted bread, layering it on and pouring any juices that have accumulated over the top. Season with flaky salt.

Top each sandwich with watercress and another piece of toast, aoili side facing in. Cut in half and serve.

Tomato Salad *with* Charred Romano Beans and Burrata

Make a caprese, but make it with some grilled beans and burrata, because it's hopefully summer where you are and you can! This dish was cobbled together one hot, heavy summer evening by the sea as an impending thunderstorm was about to hit. It did, but luckily I was able to pull together this salad off the grill just as the sky opened up. In that night's version, I quickly charred beautifully broad, flat beans on the grill because it was already in use, but here I've offered up a skillet version just in case you don't have a grill at your disposal. Either way, make this salad and eat it outside unless there is a thunderstorm happening. I would then suggest sitting indoors instead.

SERVES 4 to 6

TIME 20 minutes

INGREDIENTS

1 pound (455 g) heirloom tomatoes, cut into thick wedges (I like a mix of different colors and shapes.)

Kosher salt

2 tablespoons olive oil, plus more for drizzling

1 pound (455 g) Romano or wax beans, tipped and tailed

Freshly ground black pepper

1 (8-ounce/225 g) ball burrata, at room temperature (about 1 hour out of the fridge)

10 to 12 fresh basil leaves, for garnish

Flaky salt, for finishing

METHOD

Season the tomatoes with kosher salt and set aside.

Heat a 12-inch (30.5 cm) cast-iron skillet over medium-high for 2 minutes. Add the oil, and when it shimmers, add the beans. Cook, stirring occasionally, until they brown and blister in spots, 5 to 7 minutes, and season well with kosher salt and black pepper. Place the beans on a platter and allow them to cool for 5 minutes or so.

Quarter the burrata and distribute it evenly on the platter with the beans. Arrange the tomatoes around the cheese in any artful way that makes you happy that it's summer and you're eating tomatoes and burrata.

Scatter the salad with the basil leaves, drizzle with olive oil, and season with flaky salt.

Braised Lamb Shanks with Gingery Meyer Lemon Relish, page 205.

CHAPTER NINE

To Feed a Crowd

199–215

Just Pork Bolognese

I made this dish for Tamar when her son Louis was born. I'm not a mom, but I've seen A LOT(!), and I know how important it is to have quick meals that freeze well on hand. This is one of them. I tend to be more of a pork person than a beef person and chose to make this sauce with only that, hence the name. You could certainly swap in ground beef if you prefer, or a combination of the two, but I like it just the way it is. You'll be pleased to find it months later when you're ransacking your freezer to put dinner on the table. Bring it to a new mother and she will thank you.

SERVES 6 to 8

TIME 2½ hours

INGREDIENTS

1 medium leek, white and light green parts only, roughly chopped

1 medium carrot, roughly chopped

1 stalk celery, roughly chopped

2 cloves garlic, peeled

1 tablespoon fresh rosemary

2 tablespoons olive oil

2 tablespoons unsalted butter

Kosher salt

1 pound (455 g) ground pork

1 pound (455 g) sweet Italian sausage, casings removed

1 cup (240 ml) dry white wine

1 cup (240 ml) whole milk

2 cans (28 ounces/795 g) whole San Marzano tomatoes, crushed gently by hand

Pasta or polenta with lots of butter, for serving

Freshly grated pecorino cheese, for serving

METHOD

In a food processor, pulse together the leek, carrot, celery, garlic, and rosemary until finely chopped.

In a large skillet, heat the olive oil and the butter over medium heat. Add the chopped vegetables and cook until the leeks are translucent, about 5 minutes. Season with salt. Add the ground pork and the sausage, breaking the meat up with the back of a spoon, and cook until it is no longer pink, 7 to 9 minutes. Season with salt.

Add the white wine and cook until it evaporates, about 5 minutes, add the milk and repeat, about 5 minutes more. Add the tomatoes and stir everything together. Turn down the heat to low and gently simmer for 2 hours, adding small splashes of water, if needed, to ensure the sauce doesn't dry out. Taste and adjust seasonings accordingly.

Serve with pasta tossed with butter or over polenta with, you guessed it, even more butter stirred in and plenty of grated cheese. That's how Tamar likes it and I agree.

Citrus-Braised Short Ribs *with* Herb Salad

This recipe looks to somewhat out-of-the-box braising ingredients such as oranges for acidity and gochujang (fermented Korean chili paste) for heat to give it its own unique twist. As with all good braises, layering flavors is key. Here I have chosen to use red onion, fennel, and garlic as my mirepoix, but it's not going to "break" the recipe if you use a yellow onion, a leek, or don't have fennel around. The most important part is that you brown your short ribs well, submerge them in liquid, and then leave them alone to do their thing until the meat is falling off the bone. To serve, you can choose to shred the meat or keep the short ribs whole. I top this dish with an herb salad tossed with a touch of rice wine vinegar to give the richness of this dish a bright lift.

SERVES 6

TIME 2½ to 3 hours

INGREDIENTS

FOR THE SHORT RIBS:

5 pounds (2.26 kg) bone-in short ribs, about 1½-inch -thick

Kosher salt and freshly ground black pepper

2 tablespoons grapeseed or other high-heat neutral oil

1 medium red onion, roughly chopped (a yellow one is fine too)

1 medium fennel bulb, cored, and roughly chopped

1 head garlic, halved crosswise

1 tablespoon gochujang (Korean chili paste)

1 cup (240 ml) red wine

1 (14.5-ounce/415 g) can whole San Marzano tomatoes

1 orange, cut into wedges, rinds on

4 cups (960 ml) beef or chicken stock

FOR THE HERB SALAD:

¾ cup (30 g) fresh cilantro leaves

¾ cup (40 g) torn fresh mint leaves

⅓ cup (35 g) thinly sliced green onions (green parts only)

1 shallot, thinly sliced

2 tablespoons rice wine vinegar

¼ cup (60 ml) grapeseed or other neutral oil

Flaky salt, for finishing

Steamed rice or roasted potatoes, for serving

(Continued)

METHOD

Preheat the oven to 350°F (175°C). Season the short ribs well with kosher salt and black pepper. If you can do this the day before and refrigerate the ribs uncovered overnight even better, but regardless, let the ribs sit at room temperature for 45 minutes. You want to sear your meat when it's room temperature. Heat the oil in a large Dutch oven or heavy-bottomed, deep-sided skillet over medium-high heat. Add the short ribs and cook until deep golden brown on all sides, 8 to 10 minutes total. Set aside on a plate.

Turn down the heat to medium and add the onion, fennel, and garlic and cook until the vegetables begin to soften and turn golden brown in spots, 3 to 4 minutes. Add the gochujang and stir until the vegetables are evenly coated, about 30 seconds more. Pour in the wine, bring to a simmer, and cook until the liquid is reduced by half, 3 to 4 minutes.

Add the short ribs back to the pan. Add the tomatoes, orange wedges, and stock and bring to a simmer. Cover and braise in the preheated oven until the meat is falling off the bone, 2 to 2½ hours.

Remove the short ribs from the braising liquid and strain it. Return the liquid to the pot and discard the solids. Cook the liquid down over medium-low heat, stirring frequently, until slightly thickened and glossy, 10 to 15 minutes.

Meanwhile, prepare the herb salad: Combine the cilantro, mint, green onions, shallots, vinegar, and grapeseed oil in a bowl and toss to coat. Season with flaky salt and set aside.

Add the short ribs back to the pot and toss to coat them in the sauce. Plate them on a platter and spoon the herb salad on top. Serve with steamed rice or roasted potatoes.

Braised Lamb Shanks *with* Gingery Meyer Lemon Relish

You would be hard pressed to find a more satisfying cooking technique than braising. Tough cuts of meat are browned, bathed, and then given some alone time where they turn into tender, falling-off-the-bone brilliance. Here I've used garam masala, coriander, and cardamom to give it an Indian lean and it plays nicely with the Gingery Meyer Lemon Relish. You'll want to generously top your dish with this as well as anything else interesting that might cross your path (ahem, plate).

SERVES 4 to 8

TIME About 2½ hours

INGREDIENTS

FOR THE LAMB:

4 meaty lamb shanks (about 4 pounds/1.8 kg)

Kosher salt and freshly ground black pepper

2 tablespoons canola oil or other neutral oil, such as grapeseed

2 tablespoons olive oil

2 small red onions, peeled and quartered

3 cloves garlic, finely chopped

1½ teaspoons garam masala

1½ teaspoons ground coriander

1½ teaspoons ground cardamom

1 tablespoon tomato paste

4 cups (960 ml) chicken or beef stock

FOR THE RELISH:

1 small shallot, minced

1 small Meyer lemon, minced, rind and all

1 tablespoon grated fresh ginger

½ cup (20 g) roughly chopped, loosely packed fresh cilantro (leaves and tender stems)

⅓ cup (75 ml) olive oil

Kosher salt

Polenta, orzo, or mashed potatoes, for serving

METHOD

Season the lamb shanks with the salt and pepper. If you have the time, do this the night before and refrigerate. If not, season and let them sit at room temperature for 30 to 45 minutes before you brown them.

(Continued)

In a large Dutch oven or other heavy-bottomed, deep-sided skillet, heat the oil over medium-high heat. Brown the lamb shanks in the oil very well on all sides, about 7 minutes. Remove and set aside on a plate.

Wipe out or clean the skillet and heat the olive oil over medium heat. Add the red onions and cook until softened, about 3 minutes. Add the garlic, garam masala, coriander, and cardamom and cook until fragrant, 30 seconds more. Stir in the tomato paste and cook for an additional 30 seconds more.

Add the lamb and any accumulated juices back to the pan and pour in the stock. Bring the mixture to a boil, cover, and then simmer over low heat, flipping the lamb occasionally until the meat is tender and falling off the bone, 1½ to 2 hours.

When the lamb is nearly done, make the relish: In a bowl, mix together the shallot, lemon, ginger, cilantro, and olive oil. Season with salt to taste and set aside.

Remove the lamb to a plate and cover with foil to keep it warm. Simmer the liquid left in the pan for 10 to 15 minutes more until it thickens. Strain if you please. Plate the lamb, spoon the sauce over the shanks, and top with the relish. Serve with polenta, orzo, or mashed potatoes. Pass the remaining relish at the table. You'll want it on everything.

A NOTE: *Any extra relish would be a lovely condiment for leftover roast chicken or thinly sliced pork pressed between slices of thick, crusty bread. Stir the relish into rice or drizzle it on roasted potatoes or soft-boiled eggs for your very own family picnic.*

Fennel-Rubbed Pork Shoulder *with* Creamy White Beans and Herb Oil

Of all the things I can cook, there is truly nothing I enjoy more than slow-roasting a pork shoulder. I mean that. I do it often during the fall and winter months, usually on a Saturday or Sunday when I can stay home all day and read and write while it cooks. It also makes the house smell very good. My other favorite thing to make on days such as these is a pot of beans. Both take patience, but little else in terms of hands-on time, and the payoff is immeasurable. Let's be honest, there isn't anything better than fancy pork and beans. Everything but the herb oil can be made a day or two in advance (making it ideal for entertaining). In fact, making it ahead would be beneficial as, with any slow roast or braise, the flavors intensify and taste even better after hanging out for awhile. If you do make it ahead, just be sure to skim off the solidified fat before gently reheating. I hope you enjoy one of my most favorite meals.

SERVES 6

TIME 3 to 4 hours

INGREDIENTS

FOR THE PORK SHOULDER:

1 tablespoon fennel seeds

½ teaspoon red pepper flakes

1 skin-on, boneless pork shoulder (3 to 4 pounds/ 1.4 to 1.8 kg)

3 to 4 teaspoons kosher salt (1 teaspoon per pound of meat)

Freshly ground black pepper

¼ cup (59 ml) chicken stock, vegetable stock, or water

Flaky salt, for serving

A Pot of Beans, made with white beans such as gigante or Royal Corona (page 118)

FOR THE HERB OIL:

½ cup (20 g) loosely packed fresh basil leaves (torn if large)

½ cup (20 g) roughly chopped, loosely packed fresh cilantro (both leaves and tender stems)

½ cup (25 g) roughly chopped fresh chives

½ cup (120 ml) olive oil

Generous squeeze of lemon juice

Kosher salt

(Continued)

METHOD

Pound the fennel seeds into a coarse powder with a mortar and pestle, or alternatively, finely chop the fennel and toss it in a bowl with the red pepper flakes. Season the pork with the salt and a generous amount of black pepper and the fennel and red pepper mixture, pressing it into the meat. If you can do this the day before and refrigerate the pork uncovered overnight, even better; regardless, allow the pork to come to room temperature before roasting, about 1 hour.

Preheat the oven to 325°F (165°C). Place the pork in a Dutch oven, fat side up. Pour your liquid of choice around the meat to keep the bottom from scorching. Cover the pot and roast until the meat is very tender and easily falls apart, 3 to 4 hours, checking on occasion to make sure the bottom isn't drying out and adding a bit of liquid if needed.

Meanwhile, make the herb oil: In a food processor, combine the basil, cilantro, and chives and pulse together until finely chopped. Add the olive oil and pulse again until the mixture is silky and emulsified. Transfer to a small bowl, stir in the lemon juice and kosher salt to taste, and set aside.

Right before serving, turn the oven to broil. Uncover the pork and cook until the fat on top is golden and crispy, 2 to 3 minutes, watching to make sure it doesn't scorch. Remove from the oven and slice or gently pull the meat apart into large pieces.

Arrange some of the beans on a platter, add pieces of the pork on top, and drizzle with some of the juice that has accumulated in the bottom of the pot. Swirl about a third of the herb oil over the top the pork and beans and season with flaky salt. Pass the remaining oil at the table so your friends can spoon more over their own portion.

A NOTE: *If you're lucky enough to have leftover pork shoulder, there are a number of ways to use it. Fold the meat into soft tortillas and top with quick-pickled red onions (page 162) roughly chopped cilantro, and a swoosh of sour cream to make tacos, or to instead make it a nacho night. You could also sauté onions and garlic, add a can of San Marzano tomatoes, then add the pork to simmer to make a quick meat sauce for pasta.*

"You'll Never Use Breadcrumbs for Your Parm *Again!*" Eggplant Parm

This version of eggplant Parm has been in my family for decades. I've truthfully never seen it prepared like this anywhere else. And while it's certainly a project meal, I promise you it's worth the effort, and I hope you make it. I usually break it into a two-day affair. Unlike other traditional recipes I've come across, there are no breadcrumbs in this version, hence its name. Instead, the eggplant gets a dredge through flour and then it's dipped in a custardy mix of egg and cheese before it's shallow-fried in olive oil. This gives the eggplant a golden, airy crispiness on the outside with a creamy center. You'll still get your crunch from putting the dish under the broiler for a few minutes before serving. If you can make it a day in advance, do. Allowing it to sit overnight will help it maintain its structure more evenly for serving. Not unlike braises, these make-ahead dishes always taste better the next day, after the ingredients have gotten some time to hang together.

SERVES 8 to 10

TIME 2½ hours

INGREDIENTS

FOR THE EGGPLANT:

8 large eggs

1¼ cups (125 g) freshly grated pecorino cheese

¼ cup (13 g) finely chopped fresh flat-leaf parsley

Freshly ground black pepper

1 cup (125 g) all-purpose flour

Kosher salt

2½ pounds (1.2 kg) eggplant (about 2 medium eggplants), cut crosswise ¼ inch thick

1½ to 2 cups (360 to 480 ml) olive oil

FOR THE SAUCE AND ASSEMBLY:

3 tablespoons olive oil

½ medium red onion, thinly sliced

5 cloves garlic, finely chopped

½ teaspoon red pepper flakes

Kosher salt

1 can (28 ounces/795 g) whole San Marzano tomatoes, gently crushed by hand

1 can (15 ounces/425 g), whole San Marzano tomatoes, gently crushed by hand

½ teaspoon dried oregano

8 ounces (225 g) freshly grated low-moisture mozzarella, such as the Polly-O brand

¾ cup (70 g) freshly grated pecorino cheese

8 ounces (225 g) fresh mozzarella, thinly sliced

¼ cup (10 g) loosely packed basil, chiffonaded (leaves tightly rolled and cut into thin ribbons)

(continued)

METHOD

Make the eggplant: In a large bowl, whisk together the eggs, pecorino, and parsley and season with black pepper. Put the flour in another large bowl and season very well with salt.

Heat ¾ cup to 1 cup (180 to 240 ml) of the oil over medium-high heat in a deep-sided 12-inch (30.5 cm) skillet. Working one at a time, dredge the eggplant slices in the flour and shake off the excess. Then dip them in the egg and cheese mixture, allowing the excess to drip off. Working in batches, add the eggplant to the hot oil in one layer, giving each piece enough space so that it doesn't bump its neighbor. Fry until golden and custardy then flip and cook the other side, about 4 minutes total. Remove and place on a wire rack lined with paper towels. Season with salt. Working in batches, repeat with the remaining eggplant slices, heating the rest of the oil and wiping out the skillet as needed with a paper towel.

Make the sauce: Heat the oil in a large Dutch oven or a deep-sided 12-inch (30.5 cm) skillet. Add the onions, and cook until they have softened, 3 to 5 minutes. Add the garlic and red pepper flakes and cook 1 minute more. Season with salt. Add the tomatoes and the oregano and stir together to combine. Simmer the sauce, allowing the flavors to come together, for 20 to 25 minutes more. Taste, adjust seasoning with salt, and allow to cool slightly, 10 to 15 minutes.

Assemble the Parm: Preheat the oven to 350°F (175°C). In a bowl, toss together the grated mozzarella and pecorino. Ladle 1 cup (240 ml) of the tomato sauce into a 9 by 13-inch (23 by 33-cm) baking dish, spreading the sauce out with the bottom of the ladle to cover the bottom of the pan. Top with one layer of eggplant, overlapping the slices slightly if needed, and top with another cup (240 ml) of the sauce. Sprinkle with one-third of the cheese mixture and repeat with the remaining eggplant, sauce, and cheese. Cover the pan tightly with foil and bake for 45 to 55 minutes, until the eggplant and sauce are bubbling.

Turn the heat to 450°F (230°C). Remove and set aside the foil to cover leftovers, top the eggplant with the fresh mozzarella, and bake for another 5 to 10 minutes, until the cheese is brown and bubbling in spots, checking frequently to make sure it's not burning. Allow the eggplant parm to rest for 30 to 45 minutes (it will still be warm). Scatter with basil and serve.

Moroccan-Spiced Roast *with* Chickpeas and Herbs

This pot roast (yes, pot roast) relies on warming Middle Eastern spices such as cumin, turmeric, and cinnamon that are toasted for depth of flavor. This hearty dish is best eaten at the end of a very cold day with lots of friends sitting around the table, elbows bumping as you all reach for seconds.

SERVES 6

TIME 3½ to 4 hours

INGREDIENTS

1 chuck roast (3½ to 4 pounds/1.6 to 1.8 kg)

3½ to 4 teaspoons kosher salt and freshly ground black pepper

2 tablespoons grapeseed or canola oil

1 large yellow onion, roughly chopped

2 large carrots, diced

2 tablespoons harissa paste (I like the Belazu brand.)

3 cloves garlic, finely chopped

1 teaspoon ground cumin

1 teaspoon ground turmeric

1 cinnamon stick

3 to 4 cups (720 to 960 ml) beef stock

2 cans (15 ounces/430 g each) chickpeas, drained and rinsed

¼ cup (10 g) roughly chopped, loosely packed fresh cilantro (both leaves and tender stems)

¼ cup (13 g) roughly chopped fresh mint leaves

Pearled couscous, for serving

METHOD

Preheat the oven to 325°F (165°C). Season the meat well with salt and pepper. Allow the meat to come to room temperature.

Heat a large Dutch oven with a lid over medium-high heat. Add the oil, and when it shimmers, add the roast fat side down and let it brown. Continue browning the meat on all sides, around 10 to 12 minutes. Set aside on a plate.

Lower the heat to medium, add the onion and carrots to the pot, and cook, stirring occasionally, until softened, 4 to 5 minutes, then season with salt. Stir in the harissa and allow it to toast slightly until it turns a dark red, 1 to 2 minutes, then stir to combine. Add the garlic, cumin, and turmeric and cook 1 minute more. Season with salt. Add the meat back to the pan with the cinnamon stick and pour in enough of the broth to submerge the meat halfway. Bring to a boil, cover, and braise in the preheated oven until the meat is falling apart, 3 to 3½ hours.

Remove the meat to a plate, add the chickpeas to the pot, and cook over medium heat, until warmed through, 1 to 2 minutes. Add the meat and shred. Taste and adjust the seasoning with more salt if needed. Plate the roast and the vegetables in bowls over pearled couscous and scatter with the herbs.

CHAPTER TEN

Please Bring Dessert

217-247

Please Bring Dessert

I'm not a dessert person. I would much rather
have an amaro (or another brown spirit deemed
appropriate) and some runny cheese to close
out dinner. I'm also not a baker, which one
could argue makes sense. Why would I try to
pursue perfection for something I don't enjoy
eating myself? (This is all about me, isn't it?)
But truthfully, more often than not, my lack
of aptitude in baking makes me feel inferior. A
cook and a writer of food things that doesn't
put dinner *and* dessert on the table effortlessly?
Oui, c'est moi.

I come from generations of women who made buttery crusts, picture-perfect pies, fluffy seed-topped biscuits, and rich chocolate cakes and somehow, I am the end of the line. I overwork dough, have the patience of a shoefly, and my attention to detail for matters such as these is nil. I'm an "on the fly" gal, in a no-fly zone.

It's not that I haven't tried. I've rolled out many a galette dough, and the rusticity of my finished product is not in question. No one would deny it's authentic, it certainly looks very "homemade." Once a year I also attempt a sour cherry pie, which usually ends in tears, as a double crust is much more challenging (all that crimping too!). Plus the fact that no matter how hard I try, I always overfill it, which leads to a smoky oven and me to a breaking point. It has been proven that the very, very best I can do is Katharine Hepburn's recipe for brownies made only on a snow day. For someone who admittedly relies too much on the outward praise of others, it is all very humbling.

My lack of baking can also be problematic when entertaining. Things potentially get awkward at the end of a meal when your host offers you nothing except for more wine. (I always have plenty.) So, in pursuit of becoming a well-rounded hostess, I've come up with ways to end a meal without turning on the oven. They also happen to make me feel European in nature (excuse me while I adjust my silk scarf) and on top of my game. They include: a bowl of clementines, blood oranges, or other in-season fruit (cherries on ice are nice), or figs that you can pull apart with your hands; bars of good-quality chocolate that you can let guests "have at"; or even a loaf of something sweet from your favorite bakery, warmed and topped with ice cream. Cracking open roasted chestnuts at the table while sipping an oloroso sherry is also tip top.

But, if a guest cheerfully asks, "What can I bring?," I will always answer honestly, "Please bring dessert." Because, in fact, I do have friends that truly enjoy making and eating it. (Fine, I'll have a small piece with whipped cream.) And, if you too do not bake or don't bake well, I suggest you feel no shame, give in, and do the same. That way, everyone's a winner.

Dregs and Fruit Crumble
Daniela Galarza

I occasionally have leftover wine after a dinner party, and when I do, I save it for my next braise or marinade. But if a meaty stew isn't in the cards, the wine can be used to liven up fruit for a buttery fruit crumble. In the winter, when I tire of apples, prunes make a nice crumble after a quick plumping in red wine. In the summer months, peaches and white wine or rosé meld together nicely under a brown sugar–almond crumble hat. —D.G.

SERVES 4 to 6

TIME 55 minutes

INGREDIENTS

FOR THE FRUIT:

4 cups (620 g) pitted and roughly chopped peaches, nectarines, plums, cherries, berries, apples, or any combination (from 2 pounds/900 grams fruit)

½ cup (120 ml) leftover white wine or rosé

¼ cup (55 g) packed light brown sugar

4 teaspoons cornstarch

1 teaspoon salt

Zest of 1 lemon, plus 1 tablespoon lemon juice

FOR THE TOPPING:

¾ cup (1½ sticks/170 g) salted or unsalted butter, at room temperature

1 cup (125 g) all-purpose flour

1 cup (115 g) almond flour (or equal quantity of any ground nut or quick-cook oats—or replace with an additional cup of all-purpose flour)

7 ounces (200 g) light brown sugar

1 teaspoon kosher salt

1 teaspoon ground cinnamon

½ teaspoon vanilla extract

Ice cream or whipped cream, for serving (optional)

METHOD

In a large, wide baking dish, combine the fruit and wine and gently stir in the light brown sugar, cornstarch, salt, and lemon zest and juice. Set aside.

In a large bowl, combine the butter, all-purpose flour, almond flour, sugar, salt, cinnamon, and vanilla. Massage the ingredients together with your fingers until large, craggy crumbs form and no large pieces of butter remain. Cover and place in the refrigerator until you're ready to bake.

Preheat the oven to 375°F (190°C). Top the fruit evenly with the crumble. There may be some leftover. Bake until the fruit juices are bubbling and the crumble topping is deeply golden brown, 40 to 50 minutes.

Serve warm or at room temperature with ice cream or whipped cream if you like.

A NOTE: *Extra crumble topping can be stored in an airtight container in the refrigerator for 1 week or in the freezer for up to 3 months.*

A Trio of Grown-Up Popsicles

Gabriella Gershenson

THIS SUMMER, I have been on a popsicle-making kick. It all started when I had a hankering for Fudgsicles, but couldn't bring myself to buy them at the grocery store. There were too many ingredients listed on the box that I couldn't get behind. Is it possible, I wondered, to make my own? A genius recipe by Alice Medrich on the website Food52 showed me that yes, yes I can. This discovery kicked off a bonanza of summer freezing, and a newly minted tradition of handing out ice pops after family meals. No matter the company, old or young, vegan or omnivore, the popsicles delighted everyone. They became the embodiment of a no-big-deal yet utterly rewarding dessert. Also, they couldn't be easier to make.

I would offer you a popsicle mold hack—I am all about shortcuts—but in this instance the easiest thing to do is spend ten dollars and buy a set of ten 3-ounce (90 ml) popsicle molds from Norpro. I love their old-school shape, they come with twenty-four popsicle sticks, and they do the job beautifully. A general note about unmolding and storing popsicles: I have found that the easiest way to release them is by holding each mold under running lukewarm water until a firm tug cleanly frees the pop. I like to wrap each one in a wax paper or a parchment sandwich sleeve and store them in an airtight container in the freezer. —G.G.

Nutella Fudgsicles

This is a fudgsicle for adults, inspired by Alice Medrich's perfect recipe. Quality cocoa, Nutella (or in my case, Nocciolata, my preferred chocolate-hazelnut spread, which is organic, made without palm oil, and tastes great), and a nip of alcohol all up the intensity of this super-chocolatey, not-too-sweet pop. I use a mixture of Armagnac and amaretto, which heightens the hazelnut flavor.

MAKES　Ten 3-ounce (90 ml) ice pops

TIME　40 minutes, plus freezing time

INGREDIENTS

¼ cup (50 g) sugar

½ cup (50 g) high-quality unsweetened cocoa powder

1½ tablespoons cornstarch

2½ cups (600 ml) whole milk

½ cup (155 g) chocolate-hazelnut spread, such as Nutella or Nocciolata

1 tablespoon liquor and/or liqueur, such as Armagnac, cognac, or amaretto

Kosher salt

METHOD

Whisk together the sugar, cocoa, and cornstarch in a medium pot. Stir in enough milk to make a paste, then add the remaining milk and whisk until thoroughly combined.

Heat the mixture over medium heat, whisking constantly and scraping the bottom and sides of the pot, until small bubbles form around the edges, about 4 minutes. Cook for another 2 minutes, stirring constantly. The mixture will start to thicken and coat the sides of the pot. Remove from heat and transfer to a 32-ounce (1 liter) measuring cup.

Pour some of the hot liquid into a small bowl with the chocolate-hazelnut spread. Stir together until fully combined, then add the contents of the small bowl to the milk mixture in the measuring cup. Add the liquor, stir to combine, and season with salt to taste. Allow the mixture to come to room temperature.

Pour into the popsicle molds, leaving ¼-inch headspace on top, and freeze until solid.

Lemon Curd Labneh Popsicles

I like to think of these as a tart, lemony answer to a Creamsicle. Labneh is an extra-thick Middle Eastern yogurt. I love it because it's even richer and tangier than Greek yogurt. If you can't find it at the grocery store (Mediterranean and international markets tend to carry it), you can make your own by mixing Greek yogurt with salt and lemon juice, then straining it through a cheesecloth or a coffee filter–lined sieve overnight. Greek yogurt will also work in this recipe, but the popsicles won't be as rich. I use jarred lemon curd, because it's easy and it's actually good!

MAKES Ten 3-ounce (90 ml) ice pops

TIME 10 minutes, plus freezing time

INGREDIENTS

12.7-ounce jar (1 cup 2 tablespoons) lemon curd, such as Bonne Maman brand

1 container (16 ounces/480 ml) labneh (about 1¾ cup plus 2 tablespoons) or whole-milk Greek yogurt

2 teaspoons packed lemon zest, plus more if needed

¼ cup (60 ml) fresh lemon juice (from 1 large lemon), plus more if needed

¾ cup (180 ml) whole milk

Pinch kosher salt, plus more to taste

METHOD

Thoroughly mix together all the ingredients in a large bowl using a whisk or an immersion blender. Taste and add more lemon juice, lemon zest, or salt if needed.

Pour into the popsicle molds, leaving ¼-inch headspace on top and freeze until solid.

Vietnamese Coffee Popsicles

These are like coffee ice cream, in popsicle form. If you're ambivalent about coconut milk, not to worry. The coconut flavor doesn't come through, but the creaminess and body of the coconut milk does. I use decaffeinated coffee since the slightest bit of caffeine keeps me up, and the flavor is still great. A pinch of cardamom transforms these into Turkish coffee pops, while cinnamon takes them in a Mexican coffee direction. To make these vegan, substitute sweetened condensed coconut milk for the sweetened condensed milk. Believe it or not, they'll come out even richer.

MAKES Ten 3-ounce (90 ml) ice pops

TIME 10 minutes, plus freezing time

INGREDIENTS

1 can (13.5 ounces/405 ml) unsweetened coconut milk (about 1⅔ cups), such as Native Forest Organic Coconut Milk

⅔ cup (225 g) sweetened condensed milk (see headnote for vegan substitution)

¾ cup (180 ml) espresso or strongly brewed coffee

Kosher salt

¼ teaspoon ground cinnamon or cardamom (optional)

METHOD

In a 32-ounce (1 liter) measuring cup, whisk together the coconut milk, sweetened condensed milk, coffee, salt, and cinnamon, if using. Taste and adjust the salt or cinnamon, as needed.

Pour into 3-ounce (90 ml) popsicle molds, leaving ¼-inch headspace on top and freeze until solid.

Cultured Butter & Tahini Cookies
Rebekah Peppler

Rebekah and I met in Paris (she's lucky enough to live there) and became fast friends. She is a very talented cookbook author and food stylist who wrote *Apéritif* and *À Table*, both about the art of eating and drinking the French way—I'm sure you can see why we got along so well. She was kind enough to create this recipe for me and I'm so pleased to share it with you—these remind me of halva in cookie form, and I couldn't stop eating them. This recipe calls for cultured butter, which means the cream ferments with live bacteria before it is churned, and it develops lovely tangy notes. It's widely available in grocery stores. —C.H.

MAKES 18 to 22 cookies

TIME 30 minutes

INGREDIENTS

2¼ cups (280 g) all-purpose flour

1 teaspoon baking powder

1 teaspoon flaky sea salt, plus more for finishing

¾ cup (1½ sticks/170 g) salted cultured butter, at room temperature

1¼ cups (250 g) sugar

1 cup (255 g) tahini

1½ teaspoons pure vanilla extract

½ cup (75 g) white sesame seeds

METHOD

Preheat the oven to 350°F (175°C). In a large bowl, whisk together the flour, baking powder, and salt.

In a stand mixer fitted with the paddle attachment, beat together the butter and 1 cup (200 g) of the sugar over medium-high speed until light and fluffy, about 1½ minutes; beat in the tahini and vanilla until combined, making sure to scrape down the sides to fully incorporate. With the mixer running on low, add the flour mixture to the tahini mixture, just until incorporated. Stir in ¼ cup (37.5 g) of the sesame seeds.

In a shallow bowl, combine the remaining ¼ cup (50 g) sugar and ¼ cup sesame seeds (37.5 g).

Portion the dough into 18 to 22 balls (1½ to 2 tablespoons each). Roll the balls in the sugar-sesame mix, pressing the sesame seeds along the sides of the balls. Place on parchment-lined baking sheets, spaced about 1½ inches (4 cm) apart. Sprinkle with flaky sea salt and bake until lightly golden, 16 to 18 minutes, rotating the pans halfway through baking. Let cool on the baking sheets as they will crumble if moved beforehand.

Apple, Walnut, and Honey Upside-Down Cake
Lidey Heuck

If chocolate cake is the little black dress of desserts, then this simple apple cake is the cozy sweater you reach for every September. With tart apples, honey, ground walnuts, cinnamon, and a splash of bourbon, it's familiar and comforting and a reminder of all the things I love about autumn. (Not least, the cozy sweaters.) An upside-down cake may sound intimidating, but this one is as easy as they come—no fancy equipment needed, just a few mixing bowls and an ovenproof skillet. —L.H.

SERVES 8

TIME 50 minutes

INGREDIENTS

7 tablespoons (100 g) unsalted butter, melted and cooled, plus 1 tablespoon to grease the pan

1 cup (125 g) all-purpose flour

¾ cup (80 g) walnut halves, very finely chopped

1 teaspoon ground cinnamon

1 teaspoon baking soda

½ teaspoon baking powder

1 teaspoon kosher salt, plus more to taste

½ cup (120 ml) honey

½ cup (100 g) sugar

1 large egg, at room temperature

1 teaspoon vanilla extract

1 tablespoon bourbon (optional)

½ cup (120 ml) buttermilk or plain yogurt

2 crisp apples, such as Fuji or Honeycrisp, cored and sliced ¼ inch thick

Flaky salt, for finishing

Vanilla ice cream or lightly sweetened whipped cream, for serving

METHOD

Preheat the oven to 350°F (175°C) and grease a 10-inch (25 cm) cast-iron skillet (or other ovenproof skillet, or 10-inch [25 cm] cake pan) with butter.

In a medium bowl, whisk together the flour, walnuts, cinnamon, baking soda, baking powder, and salt.

(Continued)

In a large bowl, combine the honey, 4 tablespoons (½ stick/55 g) of the butter, ¼ cup (50 g) of the sugar, the egg, vanilla extract, and bourbon, if using, and whisk until smooth. Whisk in the buttermilk. Add the dry ingredients to the wet ingredients and whisk until just combined. Set aside.

In a small bowl, combine the remaining 3 tablespoons butter, ¼ cup (50 g) sugar, and a pinch of salt and mix until smooth. Spread this mixture evenly over the bottom of the skillet with a spatula. Arrange the apple slices on top in slightly overlapping concentric circles.

Pour the batter over the apples and smooth the top with a spatula. Bake for 30 to 35 minutes, until a toothpick inserted into the cake comes out clean. Cool for 10 minutes in the pan, then run a paring knife around the outside of the cake and carefully invert it onto a serving platter. Sprinkle with flaky salt.

Serve warm with vanilla ice cream, or at room temperature with lightly sweetened whipped cream.

Black Bun (Gingerbread, Actually)
Kerri Culhane

A true black bun is a pastry-clad fruitcake served by the Scottish on Hogmanay, the last day of the year. Tradition holds that black bun (and whisky!) be served to the person bringing luck by setting the "first foot" across the threshold after midnight. My so-called black bun is a rich and spicy gingerbread cake, which in our house performs the same festive seasonal function without the polarizing presence of dried fruit. Blackstrap molasses will make it truly black with a pleasingly bitter tang, while regular molasses will give you a lighter and sweeter cake. Serve it with big clouds of fresh whipped cream (and whisky!). —K.C.

SERVES 8

TIME 1 hour

INGREDIENTS

1 cup molasses (use the blackstrap variety if you like strong flavors)

¼ cup (60 ml) honey

1 cup (240 ml) hot water

2½ cups (315 g) all-purpose flour

1¾ teaspoons baking soda

2 teaspoons ground cinnamon

¾ teaspoon ground cloves

½ teaspoon ground nutmeg

¼ teaspoon kosher salt (You can omit if using blackstrap molasses.)

½ cup (1 stick/115 g) unsalted butter

¼ cup (55 g) packed brown sugar

1 large egg

Whipped cream and thinly sliced candied ginger, for serving (optional)

METHOD

Preheat the oven to 350°F (175°C). Butter and line a 9-inch (23 cm) round or square cake pan with parchment paper.

In a large liquid measuring cup, mix the molasses, honey, and hot water, stirring until dissolved. In a separate bowl, combine the flour, baking soda, cinnamon, cloves, nutmeg, and salt, if using.

Cream the butter and brown sugar in a stand mixer over medium speed until light and fluffy, about 2 minutes. Add the egg and beat for a minute or 2 more, until incorporated.

With the stand mixer running on low speed, combine all the ingredients in the mixture bowl, alternating between one-third of the wet and one-third of the dry ingredients until everything is incorporated.

Pour the batter into the prepared pan. Set on a baking sheet in the oven and bake for 45 to 50 minutes. Test with a toothpick after 40 minutes. If it comes out clean, the cake is done.

Cool in the pan for 10 minutes then tip the cake out to cool on a rack. Slice and serve topped with whipped cream and candied ginger, if using.

Timmymisu (A Very Good Tiramisu)
Kelly Marges

While my husband and I were still dating, he introduced me to a dear friend of his named Tim. Tim soon became a dear friend of mine too. But early in our nascent friendship, I knew only a few things about him: He was an artist with a quick and twisty wit (like meets like!) who loved a good dinner party and adored tiramisu. He would test every version of the Italian classic that he could, whether it be wheeled out on a silver cart or displayed in a diner's sweaty glass case.

Since I love both baking and making someone fall in love with me, I decided I would learn to make the Best Tiramisu of All Time. After much trial and error, I came up with this: a version that is neither too rich, nor too difficult while flirting with being both—exactly how I like my friends. I affectionately refer to it as Timmymisu in Tim's honor. (He has deemed it "very good.") —K.M.

SERVES 10 to 12

TIME 2 hours 40 minutes (includes chilling time)

INGREDIENTS

1 quart (1 liter) freshly made espresso or double-strength coffee (about one French press worth)

4 large egg yolks

¼ cup (50 g) sugar

1 pound (455 g) mascarpone cheese

3 tablespoons Kahlúa or other coffee-flavored liqueur (Rum works too!)

2 tablespoons sambuca or other anise-flavored liqueur

30 to 36 store-bought ladyfingers or Savoiardi biscuits

1 bar (about 3.5 ounces/100 g) dark chocolate (78 percent cacao is nice)

2 cups heavy cream

2 tablespoons sugar

1 teaspoon kosher salt

Handful freshly ground coffee or espresso beans

Special equipment: a trifle bowl

METHOD

Make the espresso, pour into a bowl, and set aside. (Enjoy a tiny tipple while proceeding if you want; I do!)

In the bowl of an electric mixer with the whisk attachment, beat the egg yolks and sugar on high speed until the mixture thickens and pales, 1 to 1½ minutes. Stop the mixer and scrape the sugar from the side of the bowl as necessary. Add the mascarpone and beat on medium speed until the cheese is combined and the mixture is smooth,

(Continued)

about 1 minute. Be careful not to overbeat, or the mascarpone may split. Add the Kahlúa and sambuca and beat briefly on low speed, just long enough to incorporate. Move the mascarpone mixture to a large bowl and set aside.

Before making the whipped cream (please don't buy it—homemade makes all the difference and is so easy), clean your mixer bowl and whisk attachment and place them in the freezer for 10 to 15 minutes. (A cold bowl helps the whipped cream form.) Chop the chocolate bar while the bowl is chilling and set aside.

Put the cream, sugar, and salt in the cold mixer bowl. Using the chilled whisk attachment, beat until medium peaks begin to form, about 3 minutes. (Overbeating leads to mush.)

Using a spatula, fold the whipped cream into the mascarpone mixture until evenly incorporated.

To assemble the dessert, begin by dunking the lady fingers, two at a time, into the espresso, just long enough for them to soak, then press them together over the bowl to squeeze out excess liquid. Line the bottom of a trifle bowl with the soaked biscuits, placing them side by side against the glass to form one layer. Once the bottom of the bowl has been covered, sprinkle a layer of the chocolate over the cookies. Place about one-quarter of the cream mixture on top of the chocolate layer and spread it out evenly. Depending on the size of your trifle bowl, repeat three more times, or until the ingredients are used up.

Chill the tiramisu in the refrigerator for at least 2 hours to set. Just before serving, sprinkle with a light layer of freshly ground coffee beans.

Orange, Olive Oil, and Almond Torte
Alexandra Stafford

For as long as I can remember, I can count on finding two cakes on my mother's counter during the holiday season: an orange and olive oil cake from the *New York Times* and a butter-based almond torte from *Chez Panisse Desserts*. Dusted with confectioners' sugar, these elegant cakes never fail to receive anything but rave reviews. I've long dreamed of combining these two cakes, and the product of that union. It's got lots of bright citrus flavor, thanks to orange zest, freshly squeezed juice, and a splash of orange-flavored liqueur. The inclusion of almond flour not only gives the crumb texture but also keeps it soft and delicate. Olive oil keeps the cake moist for days, so don't be afraid to make this one ahead of time. —A.S.

SERVES 10 to 12

TIME 50 minutes

INGREDIENTS

Butter or nonstick cooking spray, for greasing the pan

3 large eggs

1 cup plus 1 tablespoon (215 g) sugar

Zest of 1 orange

¼ cup (50 g) freshly squeezed orange juice

2 tablespoons Grand Marnier

¾ cup (180 ml) olive oil

1 cup (90 g) almond flour (fill the cup lightly)

1 cup (125 g) all-purpose flour

1 teaspoon baking powder

1¼ teaspoons kosher salt

Confectioners' sugar, for serving

METHOD

Preheat the oven to 350°F (175°C). Grease a 9-inch (23 cm) round pan with butter or nonstick spray. Line the bottom with a round of parchment paper.

In a large bowl, whisk the eggs until foamy and combined, about 1 minute. Add the sugar and the orange zest and beat until slightly thickened and, when you lift the whisk from the bowl, a ribbon of the egg and sugar mixture trails behind, 2 to 3 minutes. Whisk in the orange juice, Grand Marnier, and olive oil, until combined.

In a medium bowl, whisk together the almond flour, all-purpose flour, baking powder, and salt. Add the dry ingredients to the wet ingredients and stir with a spatula to combine. Pour the batter into the prepared pan and bake for 25 to 30 minutes, or until the top feels springy to the touch and a tester inserted in the center of the cake comes out clean. Let the cake cool for 10 minutes in its baking pan, then invert onto a cooling rack.

Serve warm or at room temperature and using a fine-meshed sieve dust confectioners' sugar over top.

Peach Tart with Five-Spice Honey
Peter Som

This tart is everything you want it to be. Super easy to put together, delicious, and impressive—but in a nonchalant sort of way. Your friends will think highly of you and your baking skills when all you did was halve some peaches, unfurl some store-bought puff pastry, and turn on the oven. Don't worry about it—just accept the accolades. Also, once you make this five-spice honey, you will want to drizzle it on everything; it's sweet and gently spiced and almost caramelly, so definitely serve some extra on the side for drizzling. —P.S.

SERVES 6 to 8

TIME 30 minutes

INGREDIENTS

1 sheet store-bought puff pastry, preferably Dufour, defrosted

¼ cup (60 ml) honey

2 teaspoons five-spice powder

5 small peaches, halved and pitted (After assembly, you'll have one peach half leftover to snack on.)

6 thyme sprigs

⅓ cup (45 g) roughly chopped pistachios

1 tablespoon Demerara sugar

Flaky salt and freshly ground black pepper

Vanilla ice cream, for serving (optional)

METHOD

Preheat the oven to 400°F (205°C).

Place a silicone baking liner on top of a rimmed sheet pan and unroll the puff pastry on top. Using a fork, gently prick the puff pastry all over. This is to keep the puff pastry thin and flaky versus puffy.

In a small bowl, combine the honey and the five-spice powder and microwave for 20 seconds to thin it out.

Arrange the peaches on the pastry cut side down in a three-by-three grid. Brush the fruit liberally with the five-spice honey.

Place the thyme sprigs on the tart and evenly sprinkle the pistachios and then the Demerara sugar over the top. Bake for 20 to 25 minutes, or until the pastry is puffed around the edges and golden brown.

Warm any remaining five-spice honey to loosen it again. Remove the tart from the oven and place on a plate or platter and drizzle the honey over the top. Season with flaky salt and a few turns of black pepper and serve with vanilla ice cream. Eat immediately.

Rhubarb Mess with Bay and Cardamom
Tara Donne

I love a wabi-sabi kind of dessert—the type that impresses through taste and beauty but is forgiving in technique and presentation. A mess is perfect for someone like me: a way more solid cook than baker, but also the kind of gal who prefers to show up at a friend's dinner party with something homemade and gorgeous. It took some playtime in the kitchen over the years for me to realize the range that rhubarb has. It took even longer to conclude that it doesn't require the support of a berry! As my sweet tooth leaned away from sugary desserts, the tart and vegetal qualities of rhubarb resonated more and more. This dessert is a reflection of where rhubarb and I currently stand. Fresh bay and cardamom add citrusy, herbal notes that don't attempt to overpower rhubarb's true nature with sweetness. It's great as a fool without the meringue if you're feeling lazy or pressed for time, but I really love the added texture the meringue provides. You can also make the meringue a day or two ahead and store it in a cool, dry place if you want to get ahead of the game. —T.D.

SERVES 6 to 8

TIME 2½ hours

INGREDIENTS

FOR THE MERINGUE:

3 large eggs

Pinch kosher salt

¾ cup (150 g) superfine sugar

1 teaspoon cornstarch

FOR THE COMPOTE:

1 vanilla bean

½ cup (100 g) sugar

1½ pounds (680 g) trimmed rhubarb, cut into 1-inch (2.5 cm) pieces

8 fresh bay leaves

FOR THE WHIPPED CREAM:

Time: 5 minutes

1½ cups (360 ml) heavy cream

½ teaspoon ground cardamom

2 tablespoons maple syrup

(Continued)

METHOD

Prepare the meringue: Preheat the oven to 200°F (90°C) and line a large baking sheet with parchment paper.

Carefully separate the eggs, putting the whites into a clean glass or stainless steel bowl with a pinch of salt. (Refrigerate the yolks for another use.) In a small bowl, stir together the sugar and cornstarch. Using a stand or hand mixer, beat the egg whites and salt on medium-high speed until foamy, then gradually incorporate the sugar mixture, beating constantly at high speed until a meringue forms that is glossy, sticky, and holds stiff peaks, about 4 minutes.

Spread the meringue on the prepared baking sheet in a ¼-inch-thick layer. Bake for about 1½ hours, until crisp and dry. Turn off the oven, then crack the oven door, and let the meringue cool in the oven completely, about 1 hour. Remove it from the parchment and break into 1½- to 2-inch pieces. Set aside.

Make the compote: Preheat the oven to 325°F (165°C). In a 9 by 13-inch (23 by 33 cm) baking dish, split the vanilla bean in half and rub the vanilla bean and seeds into the sugar.

Fold each of the bay leaves a few times to release the oils. Add the rhubarb and bay leaves to the baking dish and toss to coat with the sugar. Let macerate for 15 minutes.

Tightly cover the baking dish with foil and bake for 25 to 30 minutes, until the rhubarb is soft but not falling apart. Let cool to room temperature. Discard the vanilla bean and bay leaves.

Make the whipped cream: Place the metal bowl and whisk attachment of a stand or hand mixer in the freezer to chill for 15 to 20 minutes. When chilled, beat the cream on high speed until it begins to thicken, about 2 minutes. Add the cardamom and maple syrup and beat on high speed until the cream holds soft peaks.

To serve, layer the rhubarb compote, whipped cream, and meringues on plates or in bowls or glasses.

A Lit Neapolitan
Kelly Mariani

This Italian flag–inspired spin on a Baked Alaska is more about quality ingredients and assembly, and less about cooking, which is my preferred approach to making dessert. If you don't have a kitchen torch, get one! They're fun, inexpensive, and they make you feel fierce in the kitchen. —K.M.

SERVES 8

TIME 3½ hours partially active, plus 6 hours freezing time

INGREDIENTS

1 pint (480 ml) strawberry ice cream

1 pint (480 ml) vanilla ice cream

1 pint (480 ml) pistachio ice cream

3.5 ounces or about 12 store-bought ladyfingers

1 cup (240 ml) heavy cream

1 tablespoon sugar

½ teaspoon vanilla extract

FOR THE MERINGUE:

4 large egg whites

1 cup (200 g) sugar

⅛ teaspoon cream of tartar

½ teaspoon vanilla extract

⅓ cup high-proof alcohol, such as brandy, rum, or cognac (optional)

Special equipment: kitchen torch

METHOD

Pull the strawberry ice cream from the freezer to temper for a few minutes so it's easier to scoop. Spray or wipe a loaf pan with oil and line it with plastic wrap, leaving a few inches of plastic hanging over on all sides. Cut up the strawberry ice cream to make it easier to spread and, using an offset spatula, press it in an even layer in the bottom of the loaf pan. Wrap the edges of the plastic over the top of the ice cream and press down with your hands to get an even layer. Put your pan into the freezer for about an hour to set. Repeat the process with the vanilla ice cream and then the pistachio, until you have three even layers of ice cream.

Leave the pan in the freezer after the pistachio layer has set while you prep the lady fingers. Combine the cream, sugar, and vanilla together in a shallow bowl. Soak the ladyfingers for about 30 seconds, until they're soft and hydrated but not falling apart. Unwrap the plastic covering the pistachio ice cream and top the ice cream with the soaked lady fingers; freeze until solid, about 6 hours or overnight.

(Continued)

Just before serving, make the meringue: Put about 2 inches (5 cm) of water in a saucepan and bring to a simmer. Put the egg whites, sugar, and cream of tartar in the heatproof bowl of a stand mixer and place the bowl on top of the saucepan. Whisk constantly, until the sugar is dissolved and the egg whites are warm to the touch, about 3 minutes. Transfer the bowl to the mixer fitted with a whisk attachment and whisk, starting low and working up to high speed until smooth ribbons form, and then ultimately stiff, glossy peaks, about 10 minutes. Add the vanilla and whisk to combine.

Pull the ice cream terrine from the freezer and turn it out of the loaf pan. You might need to dip the pan in warm water to loosen the sides. Working quickly, use a flexible spatula to fully cover the top and all sides of the loaf with the meringue. Try to get as much meringue as you can on there, in a relatively even layer. Once you're happy with it, use your torch to brown the meringue to your desired darkness. If you're feeling extra theatrical, pour about ⅓ cup (75 ml) high-proof alcohol into a ladle and light it with the torch. While it's still burning, carefully pour the alcohol over the meringue for an additional showy moment.

Slice, serve, and feel good about yourself for delivering dinner and a show!

Popcorn for Three

We rescued Joshie from the outskirts of Brooklyn in 2005 and he quickly became the love of our lives. Like other dogs (and people), he didn't come without baggage, but adopting him taught me a love so big it makes me tear up to even write about. I'll save our whole story for next time. Like his mama, he's not a big meat eater and he doesn't have much of a sweet tooth. He prefers radishes, celery, and sliced fennel for snacks. He also loves popcorn, which I make frequently after dinner to snack on in front of the television while we finish our wine. In the past, we would give him (or rather, he would take) small handfuls from our bowl, but Joshie at eighteen is a senior now, so these days, I make sure to pop a few extra kernels so he has a portion to snack on all for his very own. We adults have been known to top our serving with one or an assortment of seasonings, including freshly ground black pepper, Aleppo pepper, garlic salt or powder, freshly grated pecorino cheese, and red pepper flakes.

SERVES 3

TIME 5 minutes

INGREDIENTS

3 tablespoons canola or grapeseed oil

¼ cup (25 g) popcorn kernels, plus 2 tablespoons (for Joshie)

Kosher salt

METHOD

In a medium saucepan, heat the oil over medium-high heat and, when it shimmers, add two popcorn kernels and put on the lid. Once you hear them pop, add in the rest of the popcorn and put the lid back on. It will likely start popping quickly; when it does, turn the heat down to medium, shaking the pan a few times to ensure as many kernels as possible get popped. (Although, I love the half popped ones at the bottom of the pot.)

You'll know to turn it off the heat when the popping slows down tremendously. Remove the lid immediately so the popcorn doesn't start to steam and become mushy, then transfer it to a large bowl. Season liberally with kosher salt. Eat on the couch with your pup.

Photo by Chad Silver.

With Gratitude

TO THE FARMS and purveyors I'm lucky to be surrounded by in the Hudson Valley: Applestone Meat, Blue Star Farm, Hudson Wine Merchants, Montgomery Place Orchard, Tivoli Mushrooms (Devon, you are the best), Samascott Orchards, and Sparrowbush Farm.

To my editor, Holly Dolce, and creative director Deb Wood at Abrams, who trusted my vision and allowed me to make the book I wanted with support and enthusiasm. You're the loveliest.

To Rebecca Bartoshesky for having the very best eye, picking the most incredible props, and for sticking with me. To food stylists Pearl Jones, Sue Li, and Tiffany Schleigh, for making my food look so much better than I ever, ever could. Also, to P+T, for shooting amidst a pandemic on my front porch. It was still fun.

To Alaina Sullivan, for taking my ramblings and turning them into the most beautifully designed book I could have ever imagined. It brought me joy when I needed it most.

To my incredible, talented friends who contributed recipes: Kerri Culhane, G. Daniela Galarza, Gabriella Gershenson, Lidey Heuck, Michael Maness, Rebekah Peppler, Peter Som, and Alexandra Stafford.

To my Scribe family, for unwavering support: Andrew and Lia Mariani, Adam Mariani, Kelly Mariani (a dessert recipe, too!), Nora Sibley Denker, and Eugenia Ballvé.

To Becky Sternal, for telling me to write from love not for love, which allowed me to keep going and for so much more.

To the vital humans in my life who kept me afloat: Rachel Beach, Kim Bucci, Erika Campbell, Kitty Cowles, Marnie Hanel, Julia Joseph, Matthew Melewski, Laura Neilson, Melissa Poll, Sarah Raimo, Alexis Rozensweig, and Kate Tyler.

To Tara Donne, for beautiful photography, your friendship, and a gorgeous dessert.

To my dearest friends who make Hudson a home: Dan Barry and Helen Dealtry, Christopher Hanrahan, and Kelly Marages. I wouldn't have made it through without you. And to Kel, also for your dessert and whip-smart edits. Backyard rosé and front porch hangs with you all till the end of time.

To Carla Lalli Music and Leslie Robarge: Our talks kept me alive and our friendship kept me grounded.

To my papa, with so much love.

To my Chad, for everything, always. And to our Joshie, forever. ■

Index